THE NEW
DARE TO DISCIPLINE

DATE DUE

~~OCT 14 98~~			
~~MAY 14 02~~			
~~JUL 8 03~~			

DEMCO 38-297

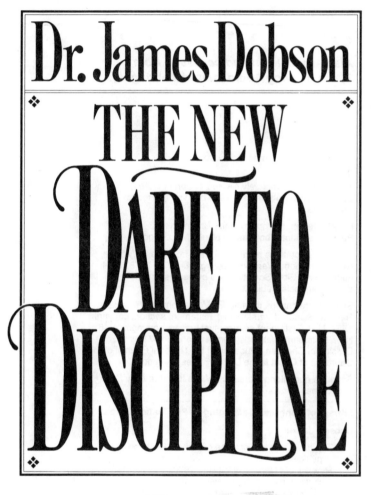

Dr. James Dobson

THE NEW DARE TO DISCIPLINE

Tyndale House Publishers, Inc.
Wheaton, Illinois

*Also available on audiocassette from
Tyndale Living Audio (material abridged).*

This book is a completely revised edition of *Dare to
Discipline,* first published in 1970 by Tyndale House
Publishers, Inc.

Back cover photo (top) by Barry Bregman
Back cover photo (bottom) by Nancy MacGregor

Scripture quotations marked NIV are from the *Holy Bible,
New International Version.* Copyright © 1973, 1978, 1984
International Bible Society. Used by permission of
Zondervan Bible Publishers.

Scripture quotations marked RSV are from the *Holy Bible,*
Revised Standard Version. Old Testament section, copyright
1952; New Testament section, first edition, copyright 1946;
New Testament section, second edition, © 1971 by the
Division of Christian Education of the National Council of the
Churches of Christ in the United States of America.

Scripture quotations marked KJV are from the *Holy Bible,*
King James Version.

Library of Congress Cataloging-in-Publication Data

Dobson, James C.,
    The new Dare to discipline / James C. Dobson.
      p. cm.
    Rev. ed. of : Dare to discipline. 1970.
    Includes bibliographical references.
    ISBN 0-8423-0507-6 (hardcover)
    ISBN 0-8423-0506-8 (softcover)
    1. Child rearing. 2. Discipline of children. I. Title.
HQ769.D58 1992
649'.64—dc20   92-17092

Printed in the United States of America

00 99 98 97 96
9   8   7   6   5   4   3   2

To Danae, Ryan, and their mother Shirley,
I affectionately dedicate the pages of this book
and the remaining years of my life.

(Written initially in 1971,
and reconfirmed more than two decades later!)

CONTENTS

❖   ❖   ❖

ONE

The Challenge

This is a book about children and those who love them. The first edition was written in the early 1970s when I was a professor of pediatrics at the University of Southern California School of Medicine. Our own children were still pre-schoolers, which made it risky to offer advice about parenting techniques. That's like a coach bragging in the first quarter about how he expects to win the game. Nevertheless, I had seen enough academically and professionally to have developed some firm convictions about how children should be raised and what they needed from their parents.

More than twenty years and 2 million copies of *Dare to Discipline* have come and gone since I first sat down to write. That passage of time has broadened my horizon and, hopefully, sharpened my vision. I've worked with thousands of families and I've considered the child-rearing views of many authorities and colleagues. My kids have paddled through adolescence and have established homes of their own. Thus, it is a special privilege for me to roll back the clock now and revisit the themes with which I first grappled so many years ago.

One might expect my views of child development and parenting to have evolved significantly within the intervening years. Such is not the case. Admittedly, the social backdrop for the original *Dare to Discipline* has changed dramatically, which is why this book needed to be revised and expanded. The student revolution that raged through the late sixties and early seventies has subsided. Woodstock and the Viet Nam War are distant memories, and university campuses are again quieter and less rebellious. But children haven't changed, nor will they ever. I'm even more convinced now that the principles of good parenting are eternal, having originated with the Creator of families. The inspired concepts in Scripture have been handed down generation after generation and are just as valid for the twenty-first century as they were for our ancestors. Unfortunately, many of today's parents have never heard those time-honored ideas and have no clue about what they're trying to accomplish at home.

I'll never forget a mother in that predicament who asked for my help in handling her defiant three-year-old daughter, Sandy. She realized that her tiny little girl had hopelessly beaten her in a contest of wills, and the child had become a tyrant and a dictator. On the afternoon prior to our conversation, an incident occurred which was typical of Sandy's way of doing business. The mother (I'll call her Mrs. Nichols) put the youngster down for a nap, but knew it was unlikely she would stay in bed. Sandy was not accustomed to doing anything she didn't fancy, and naptime was not on her list of fun things to do in the afternoon.

On this occasion, however, the child was more interested in antagonizing her mom than in merely having her own way. Sandy began to scream. She yelled loudly enough to upset the whole neighborhood, fraying Mrs. Nichols' jangled nerves. Then she tearfully demanded various things, including a glass of water.

At first Mrs. Nichols refused to comply with the orders, but she surrendered when Sandy's screaming again reached a peak of intensity. As the glass of water was delivered, the mischievous child pushed it aside, refusing to drink because her mother had not brought it soon enough. Mrs. Nichols stood offering the water for a few minutes, then said she would take it back to the kitchen if Sandy did not drink by the time she counted to five.

Sandy set her jaw and waited through the count: "three . . . four . . . five!" As Mrs. Nichols grasped the glass and walked toward the kitchen, the child screamed for the water. Sandy dangled her harassed mom back and forth like a yo-yo until she tired of the sport.

Mrs. Nichols and her little daughter are among the many casualties of an unworkable, illogical philosophy of child management which has long dominated the literature on this subject. This mother had read that a child will eventually respond to reason and forbearance, ruling out the need for firm leadership. She had been told to encourage the child's rebellion because it offered a valuable release of hostility. She attempted to implement the recommendations of the experts who suggested that she verbalize the child's feelings in a moment of conflict: "You want the water but you're angry because I brought it too late" . . . "You don't want me to take the water back to the kitchen" . . . "You don't like me because I make you take naps." She had also been taught that conflicts between parent and child were to be perceived as misunderstandings or differences in viewpoint.

Unfortunately, Mrs. Nichols and her advisors were wrong! She and her child were involved in no simple difference of opinion: she was being challenged, mocked, and defied by her daughter. No heart-to-heart talk would resolve this nose-to-nose confrontation, because the real issue was totally unrelated to water or the nap or other aspects of the particular circumstances. The actual meaning behind this conflict and a hundred others was simply this: Sandy was brazenly rejecting the authority of her mother. The way Mrs. Nichols handled these confrontations would determine the nature of their future relationship, especially during the adolescent years.

Much has been written about the dangers of harsh, oppressive, unloving discipline; these warnings are valid and should be heeded. However, the consequences of oppressive discipline have been cited as justification for the abdication of leadership. That is foolish. There are times when a strong-willed child will clench his little fists and dare his parents to accept his challenges. He is not motivated by frustration or inner hostility, as it is often supposed. He merely wants to know where the boundaries lie and who's available to enforce them.

Many well-meaning specialists have waved the banner of tolerance, but offered no solution for defiance. They have stressed the importance of parental understanding of the child, and I concur. But we need to teach children that they have a few things to learn about their parents, too!

Mrs. Nichols and all her contemporaries need to know how to set limits, and what to do when defiant behavior occurs. This disciplinary activity must take place within the framework of love and affection, which is often difficult for parents who view these roles as contradictory. *Dare to Discipline* is addressed, in part, to this vital aspect of raising healthy, respectful, happy children.

The term "discipline" is not limited to the context of confrontation, and neither is this book. Children also need to be taught *self*-discipline and responsible behavior. They need assistance in learning how to handle the challenges and obligations of living. They must learn the art of self-control. They should be equipped with the personal strength needed to meet the demands imposed on them by their school, peer group, and later adult responsibilities.

There are those who believe these characteristics cannot be taught—that the best we can do is send children down the path of least resistance, sweeping aside the hurdles during their formative years. The advocates of this laissez-faire philosophy would recommend that youngsters be allowed to fail in school if they choose . . . or maintain their bedrooms like proverbial pigpens . . . or let their puppies go hungry.

I reject this notion and have accumulated considerable evidence to refute it. Children thrive best in an atmosphere of genuine love, undergirded by reasonable, consistent discipline. In a day of widespread drug usage, immorality, sexually transmitted diseases, vandalism, and violence, we must not depend on hope and luck to fashion the critical attitudes we value in our children. Permissiveness has not simply failed as an approach to child rearing. It's been a disaster for those who have tried it.

When properly applied, loving discipline works! It stimulates tender affection, made possible by *mutual* respect between a parent and a child. It bridges the gap which otherwise separates family members who should love and trust each other. It allows the God of our ancestors to be introduced to our beloved children. It permits teachers to do the kind of job in classrooms for which they are commissioned. It encourages a child to respect other people and live as a responsible, constructive citizen.

As might be expected, there is a price tag on these benefits: they require courage, consistency, conviction, diligence, and enthusiastic effort. In short, one must *dare to discipline* in an environment of unmitigated love. We'll discuss the methods by which that can be accomplished in subsequent chapters.

TWO

Common Sense
and
Your Child

M ethods and philosophies of discipline have been the subject of heated debate and disagreement throughout the past seventy years. Psychologists and pediatricians and university professors have all gotten into the act, telling parents how to raise their kids properly. Unfortunately, many of these "experts" have been in direct contradiction with one another, spreading more heat than light about a subject of great importance.

Perhaps that is why the pendulum has swung back and forth regularly between harsh, oppressive control and the unstructured permissiveness we saw in the mid–twentieth century. It is time we realized that *both* extremes leave their characteristic scars on the lives of young victims, and I would be hard pressed to say which is more damaging.

At the oppressive end of the continuum, a child suffers the humiliation of total domination. The atmosphere is icy and rigid, and he lives in constant fear. He is unable to make his own decisions, and his personality is squelched beneath the hobnailed boot of parental authority. Lasting characteristics of dependency; deep, abiding anger; and even psychosis can emerge from this persistent dominance.

Of greater concern are the boys and girls who are being subjected to physical and emotional abuse. There are millions of families out there in which these unthinkable crimes are being committed day after day. It is hard to believe just how cruel some mothers and fathers can be to a defenseless, wide-eyed child who doesn't understand why he or she is hated. The cases I've dealt with over the years—of unloved and abused children—are impossible to forget. I remember the terrible father who regularly wrapped his small son's head in the sheet that the boy had wet the night before. Then he crammed the tot upside down into the toilet bowl for punishment. I also think of the disturbed mother who cut out her child's eyes with a razor blade. That poor little girl will go through life blind, knowing that her own mother deprived her of sight! Horrible acts like these are now occurring every day in cities and towns around us.

We should also recognize that there are many ways to abuse a child without breaking the law. It can be done subtly by ignoring a boy or girl's desperate need for nurturance. It can be accomplished by unjust and unfair punishment, including parental acts that might pass for "corporal punishment"—such as routinely hitting, slapping, kicking, and throwing the child to the ground. Then there is the entire range of humiliating behavior by a mother or father, making a youngster feel stupid and weird and unloved. Within certain limits, these behaviors are not illegal. There is no one to rescue the pitiful child who is being twisted and warped by the big people around him. Let *nothing* in this book ever hint at my approval for such tyranny.

Let me say again with the strongest emphasis that aggressive, hard-nosed, "Mommie Dearest" kinds of discipline are destructive to kids and must not be tolerated. Parents who are cold and stern with their sons and daughters often leave them damaged for life. I could easily be misunderstood at this point, having authored this book in which I recommend (in chapter 4) the judicious use of corporal punishment under specific circumstances and limits. May all doubts be dispelled. *I don't believe in parental harshness.* Period! Children are incredibly vulnerable to rejection, ridicule, criticism, and anger at home, and they deserve to grow up in an environment of safety, acceptance, and warmth.

We must acknowledge, as indicated earlier, that the opposite extreme is also damaging to children. In the absence of adult leadership, the child is his own master from his earliest babyhood. He thinks the world revolves around his heady empire, and he often has utter contempt and disrespect for those closest to him. Anarchy and chaos reign in his home, and his mother is often the most nervous, frustrated woman on her block. When the child is young, the mother is stranded at home because she is too embarrassed to take her little spitfire anywhere. It would be worth the hardships she endures if this condition produced healthy, secure children. It clearly does not.

Many of the writers offering their opinions on the subject of discipline in recent years have confused parents, stripping them of the ability to lead in their own homes. They have failed to acknowledge the desire of most youngsters to rule their own lives and prevail in the contest of wills that typically occurs between generations.

In my book *The Strong-Willed Child* I quoted from a parenting text entitled, *Your Child from Two to Five,* published during the permissive 1950s. In it was a bit of advice paraphrased from the writings of a Dr. Luther Woodward, as follows:

> What do you do when your preschooler calls you a "big stinker" or threatens to flush you down the toilet? Do you scold . . . punish . . . or sensibly take it in your stride? Dr. Woodward recommends a positive policy of understanding as the best and fastest way to help a child outgrow this verbal violence. When parents fully realize that all little tots feel angry and destructive at times, they are better able to minimize these outbursts.

Once the preschooler gets rid of his hostility, the desire to destroy is gone and instinctive feelings of love and affection have a chance to sprout and grow. Once the child is six or seven, parents can rightly let the child know that he is expected to be outgrowing sassing his parents.[1]

Having offered that sage advice, with which I disagree strongly, Dr. Woodward then told parents to brace themselves for unjust criticism. He wrote, "But this policy [of letting children engage in defiance] takes a broad perspective and a lot of composure, especially when friends and relatives voice disapproval and warn that you are bringing up a brat."

In this case, your friends and relatives will probably be right. Dr. Woodward's recommendation is typical of the advice given to parents in the mid–twentieth century. It encourages them to stand passively through the formative years when respect for authority can so easily be taught. I responded to that counsel this way in *The Strong-Willed Child*.

Dr. Woodward's suggestion is based on the simplistic notion that children will develop sweet and loving attitudes if we adults will permit and encourage their temper tantrums during childhood. According to the optimistic Dr. Woodward, the tot who has been calling his mother a"big stinker" for six or seven years can be expected to embrace her suddenly in love and dignity. That outcome is most improbable. Dr. Woodward's creative "policy of understanding" (which means stand and do nothing) offers a one-way ticket to adolescent rebellion in many cases.[2]

I believe that if it is desirable for children to be kind, appreciative, and pleasant, those qualities should be taught—

not hoped for. If we want to see honesty, truthfulness, and unselfishness in our offspring, then these characteristics should be the conscious objectives of our early instructional process. If it is important to produce respectful, responsible young citizens, then we should set out to mold them accordingly. The point is obvious: *heredity does not equip a child with proper attitudes; children learn what they are taught.* We cannot expect the coveted behavior to appear magically if we have not done our early homework.

The kind of advice Dr. Woodward and others have offered to mothers and fathers through the years has led to a type of paralysis in dealing with their kids. In the absence of "permission" to step in and lead, parents were left with only their anger and frustration in response to defiant behavior.

That thought immediately brings to mind a family I knew with four of the most unruly children I had ever met. These youngsters were the terrors of their neighborhood. They were disrespectful, loud, and aggressive. They roamed in and out of other people's garages, helping themselves to tools and equipment. It became necessary for neighbors to remove the handles from outside water faucets, because these children enjoyed leaving the water running when the families were gone.

It was interesting to observe the method of discipline used by their mother, if only because it provided a memorable example of what didn't work. Her system of controlling her brood boiled down to a simple formula. When they became too noisy or cantankerous in the backyard, she would rush out the door about once every hour and scream, "I have had it with you kids! I have just *had* it with you!" Then she would turn and go back into the house. The children never even glanced up at her. If they knew she was there they gave no indication of it. But she apparently felt it was sufficient to burst out the door like a cuckoo clock every so often and remind them she was still on the job. There must be a better way to handle the awesome task of parenting that God has assigned to us.

If both extremes are harmful, how do we find the safety of the middle ground? Surely, there is a logical, reasonable philosophy of child rearing that will guide our day-by-day interactions at home. Can't the social scientists come up with a workable game plan? Perhaps this will sound like heresy coming from a man who spent ten years of his life in behavioral and medical research, but I don't believe the scientific community is the best source of information on proper parenting techniques. There have been some worthwhile studies, to be sure. But the subject of parent-child interactions is incredibly complex and subtle. The only way to investigate it scientifically is to reduce the relationship to its simplest common denominators, so it can be examined. But in so doing, the overall tone is missed. Some things in life are so complicated that they almost defy rigorous scrutiny, and parental discipline (in my view) appears to be one of them.

The best source of guidance for parents can be found in the wisdom of the Judeo-Christian ethic, which originated with the Creator and was then handed down generation by generation from the time of Christ. This is what my mother, my grandmother, and my great-grandmother understood almost intuitively. There was within Western culture a common knowledge about children and their needs. Not everyone applied it, but most people agreed with its tenets. When a new baby was born one hundred years ago, aunts and sisters and grandmothers came over to teach the new mother how to care for her infant. What they were doing was passing along the traditional wisdom . . . the heritage . . . to the next generation, which would later perform the same service for the newcomers on the block. That system worked pretty well until the 1920s and thereafter. Slowly, the culture began to lose confidence in that tradition and shifted its allegiance to the experts. Behaviorist J. B. Watson was one of the first and most influential gurus to come along. He offered what he called a "foolproof" method of child rearing, and mothers bought it hook, line, and sinker. If only they would follow his advice, he said, they could produce any kind of a child they wanted . . . "a doctor, lawyer, artist, merchant-chief, and—yes—even a beggarman and a thief."

Watson advised parents, if they wanted the best results, to show no affection for their offspring. He wrote:

> "Never hug and kiss them, never let them sit on your lap. If you must, kiss them once on the forehead when they say good night. Shake hands with them in the morning. . . .
>
> "Remember when you are tempted to pet your child, that mother love is a dangerous instrument. An instrument which may inflict a never-healing wound, a wound which may make infancy unhappy, adolescence a nightmare, an instrument which may wreck your adult son or daughter's vocational future and their chances for marital happiness."[3]

This advice from Dr. Watson comes across today like pure nonsense, and indeed, that's just what it is. In fact, it's difficult to believe anyone gave credibility to such advice even in 1928. Yet Watson was enormously popular in his day, and his books sold in the millions. Mothers and fathers worked diligently to "condition" their children in the way recommended by this half-baked hot dog.

Then came Dr. Sigmund Freud, and Dr. Benjamin Spock, and Dr. A. S. Neill (see chapter 7), and Dr. Tom Gordon, and Dr. Ruth Westheimer, and Phil Donahue, and Oprah Winfrey, and the *Ladies' Home Journal,* and *Cosmopolitan,* and *Red-*

book, and finally, a newspaper for "enquiring minds who want to know." With every new, off-the-wall suggestion that came along, I asked myself: If their new approach to child-rearing is so wonderful, why was it not observed until now? How come 20 billion parents across more than five thousand years failed to notice the concept? Certainly, the accumulated experience of all that mothering and fathering should count for *something!*

My primary purpose in writing this book, both the 1970 version and this recomposition, has been to record for posterity my understanding of the Judeo-Christian concept of parenting that has guided millions of mothers and fathers for centuries. I am convinced that it will prove successful in *your* home, too. Let's move on, then, to examine five underpinnings to commonsense child rearing.

1. *Developing respect for parents is the critical factor in child management.* It is imperative that a child learns to respect his parents—not to satisfy their egos, but because his relationship with them provides the basis for his later attitude toward all other people. His early view of parental authority becomes the cornerstone of his future outlook on school authority, law enforcement officers, employers, and others with whom he will eventually live and work. The parent-child relationship is the first and most important social interaction a youngster will have, and the flaws and knots experienced there can often be seen later in life.

Respect for parents must be maintained for another equally important reason. If you want your child to accept your values when he reaches his teen years, then you must be worthy of his respect during his younger days. When a child can successfully defy his parents during his first fifteen years, laughing in their faces and stubbornly flouting their authority, he develops a natural contempt for them.

"Stupid old Mom and Dad! I have them wound around my little finger. Sure they love me, but I really think they're afraid of me." A child may not utter these words, but he feels them each time he outsmarts his elders and wins the confrontations and battles. Later he is likely to demonstrate his disrespect in a more blatant manner. Viewing his parents as being unworthy of his respect, he may very well reject every vestige of their philosophy and faith.

This factor is also of vital importance to Christian parents who wish to transmit their love for Jesus Christ to their sons and daughters. Why? Because young children typically identify their parents . . . and especially their fathers . . . with God. Therefore, if Mom and Dad are not worthy of respect, then neither are their morals, their country, their values and beliefs, or even their religious faith.

I was shocked to see this close identification between God and me in the mind of our son when he was two years old. Ryan had watched his mother and me pray before we ate each meal, but he had never been asked to say grace. One day when I was out of town on a business trip, Shirley spontaneously turned to the toddler and asked if he would like to pray before they ate. The invitation startled him, but he folded his little hands, bowed his head, and said, "I love you, Daddy. Amen."

When I returned home and Shirley told me what had happened, the story unsettled me. I hadn't realized the degree to which Ryan linked me with his "Heavenly Father." I wasn't even sure I wanted to stand in those shoes. It was too big a job, and I didn't want the responsibility. But I had no choice, nor do you. God has given us the assignment of representing Him during the formative years of parenting. That's why it is so critically important for us to acquaint our kids with God's two predominant natures . . . His unfathomable love and His justice. If we love our children but permit them to treat us disrespectfully and with disdain, we have distorted their understanding of the Father. On the other hand, if we are rigid disciplinarians who show no love, we have tipped the scales in the other direction. What we teach our children about the Lord is a function, to some degree, of how we model love and discipline in our relationship with them. Scary, huh?

The issue of respect is also useful in guiding parents' interpretation of given behavior. First, they should decide whether an undesirable act represents a direct challenge to their authority . . . to their leadership position as the father or mother. The form of disciplinary action they take should depend on the result of that evaluation.

For example, suppose little Chris is acting silly in the living room and falls into a table, breaking many expensive china cups and other trinkets. Or suppose Wendy loses her bicycle or leaves her mother's coffeepot out in the rain. These are acts of childish irresponsibility and should be handled as such. Perhaps the parent will ignore the event or maybe have the child work to pay for the losses—depending on his age and maturity, of course.

However, these examples do not constitute direct challenges to authority. They do not emanate from willful, haughty disobedience and therefore should not result in serious discipline. In my opinion, spankings (which we will discuss later) should be reserved for the moment a child (between the age of eighteen months to ten years old) expresses to parents a defiant "I will not!" or "You shut up!" When youngsters convey this kind of stiff-necked rebellion, you must be willing to respond to the challenge immediately. When nose-to-nose confrontation occurs between you and your child, it is not the time to discuss the virtues of obedience. It is not the occasion to send him to his room to pout. Nor is it appropriate to postpone disciplinary measures until your tired spouse plods home from work.

You have drawn a line in the dirt, and the child has deliberately flopped his bony little toe across it. Who is going to win? Who has the most courage? Who is in charge here? If you do not conclusively answer these questions for your strong-willed children, they will precipitate other battles designed to ask them again and again. It is the ultimate paradox of childhood that youngsters want to be led, but insist that their parents earn the right to lead them.

When mothers and fathers fail to take charge in moments of challenge, they create for themselves and their families a potential lifetime of heartache. That's what happened in the case of the Holloways, who were the parents of a teen named Becky (not their real names). Mr. Holloway came to see me in desperation one afternoon and related the cause for his concern. Becky had never been required to obey or respect her parents, and her early years were a strain on the entire family. Mrs. Holloway was confident Becky would eventually become more manageable, but that never happened. She held her parents in utter contempt from her youngest childhood and was sullen, disrespectful, selfish, and uncooperative. Mr. and Mrs. Holloway did not feel they had the right to make demands on their daughter, so they smiled politely and pretended not to notice her horrid behavior.

Their magnanimous attitude became more difficult to maintain as Becky steamrolled into puberty and adolescence. She was a perpetual malcontent, sneering at her family in disgust. Mr. and Mrs. Holloway were afraid to antagonize her in any way because she would throw the most violent tantrums imaginable. They were victims of emotional blackmail. They thought they could buy her cooperation, which led them to install a private telephone in her room. She accepted it without gratitude and accumulated a staggering bill during the first month of usage.

They thought a party might make her happy, and Mrs. Holloway worked very hard to decorate the house and prepare refreshments. On the appointed evening, a mob of dirty, profane teens swarmed into the house, breaking and destroying the furnishings. During the course of the evening, Mrs. Holloway said something that angered Becky. The girl struck her mother and left her lying in a pool of blood in the bathroom.

Away from home at the time, Mr. Holloway returned to find his wife helpless on the floor; he located his unconcerned daughter in the backyard, dancing with friends. As he described for me the details of their recent nightmare, he spoke with tears in his eyes. His wife, he said, was still in the hospital contemplating her parental failures as she recovered from her wounds.

Parents like the Holloways often fail to understand how love and discipline interact to influence the attitudes of a child. These two aspects of a relationship are not opposites working against each other. They are two dimensions of the same quality. One demands the other. Disciplinary action is not an assault on parental love; it is a function of it. Appropriate punishment is not something parents do *to* a beloved child; it is something done *for* him or her. That simple understanding when Becky was younger could have spared the Holloways an adolescent nightmare.

Their attitude when Becky rebelled as a preschooler should have been, "I love you too much to let you behave like that." For the small child, word pictures can help convey this message more clearly. The following is a story I used with our very young children when they crossed the line of unacceptable behavior:

I knew of a little bird who was in his nest with his mommy. The mommy bird went off to find some worms to eat, and she told the little bird not to get out of the nest while she was gone. But the little bird didn't mind her. He jumped out of the nest and fell to the ground where a big cat got him. When I tell you to mind me, it is because I know what is best for you, just as the mommy bird did with her baby bird. When I tell you to stay in the front yard, it's because I don't want you to run in the street and get hit by a car. I love you, and I don't want anything to happen to you. If you don't mind me, I'll have to spank you to help you remember how important it is. Do you understand?

My own mother had an unusually keen understanding of good disciplinary procedures, as I have indicated. She was very tolerant of my childishness, and I found her reasonable on most issues. If I was late coming home from school and I could explain what caused the delay, that was the end of the matter. If I didn't get my work done, we could sit down and reach an agreement for future action. But there was one matter on which she was absolutely rigid: She did not tolerate sassiness. She knew that backtalk and what she called "lip" were a child's most potent weapon to defiance and had to be discouraged.

I learned very early that if I was going to launch a flippant attack on her, I had better be standing at least twelve feet away. This distance was necessary to avoid an instantaneous response—usually aimed at my backside.

The day I learned the importance of staying out of reach shines like a neon light in my mind. I made the costly mistake of sassing her when I was about four feet away. I knew I had crossed the line and wondered what she would do about it. It didn't take long to find out. Mom wheeled around to grab something with which to express her displeasure, and her hand landed on a girdle. Those were the days when a girdle was lined with rivets and mysterious panels. She drew back and swung that abominable garment in my direction, and I can still hear it whistling through the air. The intended blow caught me across the chest, followed by a multitude of straps and buckles, wrapping themselves around my midsection. She gave me an entire thrashing with one blow! But from that day forward, I measured my words carefully when addressing my mother. I never spoke disrespectfully to her again, even when she was seventy-five years old.

I have shared that story many times through the years, to an interesting response. Most people found it funny and fully understood the innocuous meaning of that moment. A few others, who never met my mother and had no knowledge of her great love for me, quickly condemned her for the abusiveness of that event. One Christian psychologist even wrote a chapter in his book on the viciousness of that spanking. Another man in Wichita, Kansas, was so furious at me for telling the story that he refused to come hear me speak. Later he admitted he had misread the word girdle, thinking my mother had hit me with a *griddle*.

If you're inclined to agree with the critics, please hear me out. I am the only person on earth who can report accurately the impact of my mother's action. I'm the only one who lived it. And I'm here to tell you that the girdle-blow was an act of love! My mother would have laid down her life for me in a heartbeat, and I always knew it. She would not have harmed a hair on my fuzzy head. Yes, she was angry at my insolence, but her sudden reaction was a corrective maneuver. We both knew I richly deserved it. And that is why the momentary pain of that event did not assault my self-worth. Believe it or not, it made me feel loved. Take it or leave it, Dr. Psychologist, but that's the truth.

Now let me say the obvious. I can easily see how the same setting could have represented profound rejection and hostility of the first order. If I had not known I was loved . . . if I had not deserved the punishment . . . if I had been frequently and unjustly struck for minor offenses . . . I would have suffered serious damage from the same whirring girdle. The minor pain was not the critical variable. The *meaning* of the event is what mattered.

This single episode illustrates why it is so difficult to conduct definitive research on child-rearing practices. The critical factors are too subjective to be randomized and analyzed. That complexity also explains why social workers seeking to rescue children from abusive homes often have such problems being fair. Many good parents in loving homes have lost custody of their sons and daughters because of evidence that is misinterpreted. For example, a dime-sized bruise on the buttocks of a fair-skinned child may or may not indicate an abusive situation. It all depends. In an otherwise secure and loving home, that bruise may have had no greater psychological impact than a skinned knee or a stubbed toe. Again, the significant issue is not the small abrasion; it is the *meaning* behind it—the way it occurred and the overall tone of the relationship. Nevertheless, grief-stricken parents have lost their children on the basis of a single piece of evidence of that nature. We call it parent abuse.

Please don't write and accuse me of defending parents who routinely bruise and harm their children even in a minor way. It is wrong. It should not happen. But someone should have the courage to say we must look at the *total* relationship before removing a child from the security of a good home and not base a life-changing decision on a single bit of evidence.

Getting back to our theme of respect, let me emphasize that it will not work properly as a unilateral affair; it must run both ways. Parents cannot require their children to treat them with dignity if they will not do the same in return. Parents should be gentle with their child's ego, never belittling or embarrassing him or her in front of friends. Discipline should usually be administered away from the curious eyes of gloating onlookers. Children should not be laughed at if it makes them uncomfortable. Their strong feelings and requests, even if foolish, should be given an honest appraisal. They should feel that their parents "really *do* care about me." Self-esteem is the most fragile attribute in human nature. It can be damaged by very minor incidents, and its reconstruction is often difficult to engineer.

Thus, a father who is sarcastic and biting in his criticism of children cannot expect to receive genuine respect in return. His offspring might *fear* him enough to conceal their contempt. But revenge will often be sought in adolescence. Children know the wisdom of the old axiom, "Don't mock the alligator until you are across the stream." Thus, a vicious, toothy father may intimidate his household for a time, but if he does not demonstrate respect for its inhabitants, they may return his hostility when they reach the safety of early adulthood.

FULL-BLOWN TODDLERHOOD

Before leaving the topic of respect, let's say a few words about that marvelous time of life known as toddlerhood. It begins with a bang (like the crash of a lamp or a porcelain vase) at about eighteen months of age and runs hot and heavy until about the third birthday. A toddler is the most hard-nosed opponent of law and order, and he honestly believes the universe circles around him. In his cute little way, he is curious and charming and funny and lovable and exciting . . . and selfish and demanding, and rebellious and destructive. Comedian Bill Cosby must have had some personal losses at the hands of toddlers, for he is quoted as saying, "Give me two hundred active two-year-olds and I could conquer the world."

Children between fifteen and thirty-six months of age do not want to be restricted or inhibited in any manner, nor are they inclined to conceal their viewpoint. They resent every nap imposed on them, and bedtime becomes an exhausting, dreaded ordeal each night. They want to play with everything in reach, particularly fragile and expensive ornaments. They prefer using their pants rather than the potty, and insist on eating with their hands. And need I remind you that most of what goes in their mouths is not food. When they break loose in a store, they run as fast as their fat little legs will carry them. They pick up the kitty by its ears and then scream bloody murder when scratched. They want mommy within three feet of them all day, preferably in the role of their full-time playmate. Truly, the toddler is a tiger!

Parents who do everything right in managing these precious babies still are likely to find them hard to control. For this reason, moms and dads should not hope to make their two-year-olds act like more mature children. A controlling but patient hand will eventually succeed in settling the little anarchist, but probably not until he is between three and four. Unfortunately, however, the child's attitude toward authority can be severely damaged during his toddler years. Parents who love their cute little butterball so much that they cannot risk antagonizing him may lose and never regain his control. This is the time to establish themselves, gently but persistently, as the bosses to be reckoned with.

I once dealt with a mother of a rebellious thirteen-year-old boy who snubbed every hint of parental authority. He would not come home until at least two o'clock in the morning, and deliberately disobeyed every request she made of him. Assuming that her lack of control was a long-standing difficulty, I asked if she could tell me the history of this problem. She clearly remembered when it all started: Her son was less than three at the time. She carried him to his room and placed him in his crib, and he spit in her face.

She explained the importance of not spitting in mommy's face, but was interrupted by another moist missile. This mother had been told that all confrontations could be resolved by love, understanding, and discussion. So she wiped her face and began again, at which point she was hit with another well-aimed blast. Growing increasingly frustrated, she shook him . . . but not hard enough to disrupt his aim with the next wad.

What could she do then? Her philosophy offered no honorable solution to this embarrassing challenge. Finally, she rushed from the room in utter exasperation, and her little conqueror spat on the back of the door as it shut. She lost; he won! This exasperated mother told me she never had the upper hand with her child after that night!

When parents lose these early confrontations, the later conflicts become harder to win. Parents who are too weak or tired or busy to win make a costly mistake that will haunt them during their child's adolescence. If you can't make a five-year-old pick up his toys, it is unlikely you will exercise much control during his most defiant time of life.

It is important to understand that adolescence is a condensation or composite of all the training and behavior that have gone before. Any unsettled matter in the first twelve years is likely to fester and erupt during adolescence. The proper time to begin disarming the teenage time-bomb, then, is twelve years before it arrives. As Dr. Bill Slonecker, a Nashville pediatrician and very good friend, said on a "Focus on the Family" radio broadcast, "If discipline begins on the second day of life, you're one day late."

Dr. Slonecker wasn't referring to spanking a baby or any other physical discipline per se. Rather, he was speaking of parents being in charge—loving the child enough to establish control. All too often he saw mothers in his private practice who were afraid to lead their infants. They would call his office and frantically huff, "My six-month old baby is crying and seems very hot." He would ask the women if the child had a fever, to which they would reply, "I don't know. He won't let me take his temperature." Those mothers had already yielded some of their authority to their infants. They would live to regret it.

I must point out that some rebellious behavior is distinctly different in origin from the "challenging" defiance I've been describing. A child's antagonism and stiff-lipped negativism may emanate from frustration, disappointment, or rejection, and must be interpreted as a warning signal to be heeded. Perhaps the toughest task in parenthood is recognizing the difference between these two distinct motives.

A child's resistant behavior always contains a message to his parents, which they must decode before responding. That message is often phrased in the form of a question: "Are you in charge or am I?" A distinct reply is appropriate to discourage future attempts to overthrow constituted government in the home. On the other hand, Junior's antagonism may be his way of saying, "I feel unloved now that I'm stuck with a yelling baby brother. Mom used to care for me; now nobody wants me. I hate everybody." When this kind of meaning underlies the rebellion, parents should move quickly to pacify its cause.

The most effective parents are those who have the skill to get behind the eyes of their child, seeing what he sees, thinking what he thinks, feeling what he feels. For example, when a two-year-old screams and cries at bedtime, one must ascertain what he is communicating. If he is genuinely frightened by the blackness of his room, the appropriate response should be quite different than if he is merely protesting about having to go nighty-night. The art of good parenthood revolves around the interpretation of meaning behind behavior.

If parents intuitively *know* their child, they will be able to watch and discern what is going on in his little head. The child will *tell* them what he is thinking if they learn to listen carefully. Unless they can master this ability, however, they will continually fumble in the dark in search of a proper response.

Repeating the first point, the most vital objective of disciplining a child is to gain and maintain his respect. If the parents fail in this task, life becomes uncomfortable indeed. We'll move on now to the other four elements of a traditional approach to child rearing, discussed in the next chapter.

THREE

More Common Sense about Children

I indicated in the first chapter that there were certain risks associated with my being a young father and simultaneously choosing to write and speak about the discipline of children. That placed enormous pressure on our imperfect family in those days. But God gave me good kids and we handled the fishbowl experience rather well. There were a few tough moments, however, that proved to be quite embarrassing.

One of those nightmares occurred on a Sunday evening in 1974, when Danae was nine and Ryan nearly five. I was asked to speak on that occasion in a church service near our home. As it turned out, I made two big mistakes that night. First, I decided to speak on the discipline of children, and second, I brought my kids to the church with me. I should have known better.

After I had delivered my thought-provoking, witty, charming, and informative message that evening, I stood at the front of the sanctuary to talk to parents who sought more advice. Perhaps twenty-five mothers and fathers gathered around, each asking specific questions in turn. There I was, dispensing profound child-rearing wisdom like a vending machine, when suddenly we all heard a loud crash in the balcony. I looked up in horror to see Danae chasing Ryan over the seats, giggling and stumbling and running through the upper deck. It was one of the most embarrassing moments of my life. I could hardly go on telling the lady in front of me how to manage her children when mine were going crazy in the balcony; nor could I easily get my hands on them. I finally caught Shirley's eye and motioned for her to launch a seek-and-destroy mission on the second tier. Never again did I speak on that subject with our kids in tow.

I share that story to clarify the goal of proper child rearing. It is not to produce perfect kids. Even if you implement a flawless system of discipline at home, which no one in history has done, your children will be children. At times they will be silly, destructive, lazy, selfish, and—yes—disrespectful. Such is the nature of humanity. We as adults have the same problems. Furthermore, when it comes to kids, that's the way it *should* be. Boys and girls are like clocks; you have to let them run. My point is that the principles in this book are not designed to produce perfect little robots who can sit with their hands folded in the parlor thinking patriotic and noble thoughts! Even if we *could* pull that off, it wouldn't be wise to try.

The objective, as I see it, is to take the raw material with which our babies arrive on this earth, and then gradually mold it into mature, responsible, and God-fearing adults. It is a twenty-year process that will bring progress, setbacks, successes, and failures. When the child turns thirteen, you'll swear for a time that he's missed everything you thought you had taught . . . manners, kindness, grace, and style. But then, maturity begins to take over and the little green shoots from former plantings start to emerge. It is one of the richest experiences in living to watch that progression from infancy to adulthood in the span of two dynamic decades.

Let's move on now to discuss the remaining four principles in the commonsense approach to child rearing.

2. *The best opportunity to communicate often occurs after a disciplinary event.* Nothing brings a parent and child closer together than for the mother or father to win decisively after being defiantly challenged. This is particularly true if the

child was "asking for it," knowing full well he deserved what he got. The parents' demonstration of their authority builds respect like no other process, and the child will often reveal his affection after the initial tears have dried.

For this reason, parents should not dread or shrink back from confrontations with their children. These occasions should be anticipated as important events, because they provide the opportunity to convey verbal and nonverbal messages to the boy or girl that cannot be expressed at other times. Let me again stress that I am not suggesting that parents use excessive punishment in these encounters. To the contrary, a small amount of discomfort goes a long way toward softening a child's rebellious spirit. However, the spanking should be of sufficient magnitude to cause genuine tears.

After emotional ventilation, the child will often want to crumple to the breast of his parent, and he should be welcomed with open, warm, loving arms. At that moment you can talk heart to heart. You can tell him how much you love him, and how important he is to you. You can explain why he was disciplined and how he can avoid the difficulty next time. This kind of communication is often impossible with other disciplinary measures . . . such as standing the youngster in the corner or taking away his favorite toy. A resentful child usually does *not* want to talk.

A confrontation my wife once had with our daughter, Danae, can illustrate the point. Back when Danae was but a fifteen-month-old ankle-biter, Shirley wanted to build a fire in the fireplace and needed to go out behind the garage to get some wood. It was raining, so she told Danae, who was barefoot, to wait in the doorway. Having learned to talk quite early, Danae knew the meaning of the command. Nevertheless, she suddenly came skipping across the wet patio. Shirley caught her and took her back, repeating the order more sternly. But as soon as Shirley's back was turned, Danae scooted out again. It was an unmistakable act of disobedience to a clear set of instructions. Then, on the third trip, Shirley stung Danae's little legs a few times with a switch.

After her tears had subsided, the toddler came to Shirley by the fireplace and reached out her arms, saying "Love, Mommy." Shirley gathered Danae tenderly in her arms and rocked her for fifteen minutes. During those loving moments, she talked softly with her about the importance of obedience.

Parental warmth after such discipline is essential to demonstrate that it is the *behavior*—not the child himself—that the parent rejects. William Glasser, the father of Reality Therapy, made this distinction very clear when he described the difference between discipline and punishment. "Discipline" is directed at the objectional behavior, and the child will accept its consequence without resentment. He defined "punishment" as a response that is directed at the individual. It represents a desire of one person to hurt another; and it is expression of hostility rather than corrective love. As such, it is often deeply resented by the child.

Although I sometimes use these terms interchangeably, I agree with Glasser's basic premise. Unquestionably, there is a wrong way to correct a child that can make him or her feel unloved, unwanted, and insecure. One of the best guarantees against this happening is a loving conclusion to the disciplinary encounter.

3. *Control without nagging (it is possible).* Yelling and nagging at children can become a habit, and an ineffectual one at that! Have you ever screamed at your child, "This is the last time I'm telling you for the last time!" Parents often use anger to get action instead of using action to get action. It is exhausting and it doesn't work! Trying to control children by screaming is as utterly futile as trying to steer a car by honking the horn.

Let's consider an illustration that could represent any one of a million homes at the end of a long, intense, whirlwind day. Dead-tired, Mom feels her head pounding like a bass drum as she contemplates getting her son to take a bath and go to bed. But eight-year-old Henry does not *want* to go to bed and knows from experience that it will take his harassed mother at least thirty minutes to get him there.

Henry is sitting on the floor, playing with his games. Mom looks at her watch and says, "Henry, it's nearly nine o'clock (a thirty-minute exaggeration), so gather up your toys and go take your bath." Now Henry and Mom both know that she didn't mean for him to *immediately* take a bath. She merely wanted him to start *thinking* about taking his bath. She would have fainted dead away if he had responded to her empty command.

Approximately ten minutes later, Mom speaks again. "Now, Henry, it's getting later and you have school tomorrow; I want those toys picked up and then I want you in that tub!" She still does not intend for Henry to obey, and he knows it. Her *real* message is, "We're getting closer, Hank." Henry shuffles around and stacks a box or two to demonstrate that he heard her. Then he settles down for a few more minutes of play.

Six minutes pass and Mom issues another command, this time with more passion and threat in her voice, "Now listen, young man, I told you to get a move on, and I meant it!" To Henry, this means he must get his toys picked up and m-e-a-n-d-e-r toward the bathroom door. If his mother rapidly pursues him, then he must carry out the assignment posthaste. However, if Mom's mind wanders before she performs the last step of this ritual, or if the phone miraculously rings, Henry is free to enjoy a few minutes' reprieve.

You see, Henry and his mother are involved in a familiar one-act play. They both know the rules and the role being enacted by the opposite actor. The entire scene is preprogrammed, computerized, and scripted. In actuality, it's a virtual replay of a scene that occurs night after night. Whenever Mom wants Henry to do something he dislikes, she progresses through graduated steps of phony anger, beginning with calmness and ending with a red flush and threats. Henry does not have to move until she reaches her flashpoint.

How foolish this game is. Since Mom controls Hank with empty threats, she must stay half-irritated all the time. Her relationship with her children is contaminated, and she ends each day with a pulsing migraine above her left eye. She can never count on instant obedience, because it takes her at least five minutes to work up a believable degree of anger.

How much better it is to use *action* to achieve the desired behavior. There are hundreds of approaches that will bring a desired response, some of which involve slight pain, while others offer the child a reward. The use of rewards or "positive reinforcement" is discussed in the next chapter, and thus will not be presented here. But minor pain or "negative reinforcement" can also provide excellent motivation for the child.

When a parent's calm request for obedience is ignored by a child, Mom or Dad should have some means of making their youngster *want* to cooperate. For those who can think of no such device, I will suggest one: it is muscle lying snugly against the base of the neck. Anatomy books list it as the trapezius muscle, and when firmly squeezed, it sends little messengers to the brain saying, "This hurts: avoid recurrence at all costs." The pain is only temporary; it can cause no damage. But it is an amazingly effective and practical recourse for parents when their youngster ignores a direct command to move.

Let's return to the bedtime scene with Henry, and let me suggest how it could be replayed more effectively. To begin, his mother should have forewarned him that he had fifteen more minutes to play. No one, child or adult, likes a sudden interruption of his activity. It then would have been wise to set the alarm clock or the stove buzzer. When the fifteen minutes passed and the buzzer sounded, Mom should have quietly told Henry to go take his bath. If he didn't move immediately, his shoulder muscle could have been squeezed. If Henry learns that this procedure or some other unpleasantry is invariably visited upon him, he will move before the consequences ensue.

I know that some of my readers could argue that the deliberate, premeditated application of minor pain to a small child is a harsh and unloving thing to do. To others, it will seem like pure barbarism. I obviously disagree. Given a choice between a harassed, screaming, threatening mother who blows up several times a day versus a mom who has a reasonable, controlled response to disobedience, I would certainly recommend the latter. In the long run, the quieter home is better for Johnny, too, because of the avoidance of strife between generations.

On the other hand, when a youngster discovers there is no threat behind the millions of words he hears, he stops listening to them. The only messages he responds to are those reaching a peak of emotion, which means there is much screaming and yelling going on. The child is pulling in the opposite direction, fraying Mom's nerves and straining the parent-child relationship. But the most important limitation of those verbal reprimands is that their user often has to resort to physical punishment in the end anyway. It is also more likely to be severe, because the adult is irritated and out of control. Thus, instead of the discipline being administered in a calm and judicious manner, the parent has become unnerved and frustrated, swinging wildly at the belligerent child. There was no reason for a fight to have occurred. The situation could have ended very differently if the parental attitude had been one of confident serenity.

Speaking softly, almost pleasantly, Mom says, "Henry, you know what happens when you don't mind me; now I don't see any reason in the world why I should have to make you uncomfortable just to get your cooperation tonight, but if you insist, I'll play the game with you. When the buzzer sounds you let me know what the decision is."

The child then has the choice to make, and the advantages to him of obeying his mother's wishes are clear. She need not scream. She need not threaten to shorten his life. She need not become upset. She is in command. Of course, Mother will have to prove two or three times that she will apply the pain or other punishment, if necessary. Occasionally throughout the coming months, Henry will check to see if she is still at the helm. That question is easily answered.

The shoulder muscle is a surprisingly useful source of minor pain. It can be utilized in those countless situations where face-to-face confrontations occur between adult and child. One such incident happened to me back in the days when my own kids were young. I had come out of a drugstore, and there at its entrance was a stooped, elderly man, approximately seventy-five or eighty years of age. Four boys, probably ninth graders, had cornered him and were running circles around him. As I came through the door, one of the boys had just knocked the man's hat down over his eyes and they were laughing about how silly he looked, leaning on his cane.

I stepped in front of the elderly fellow and suggested that the boys find someone else to torment. They called me names and then sauntered off down the street. I got in my car and was gone about fifteen minutes. I returned to get something I had forgotten, and as I was getting out of my car I saw the same four boys running from a nearby hardware store. The proprietor raced after them, shaking his fist and screaming in protest. I discovered later that they had run down the aisles in his store, raking cans and bottles off the shelves and onto the floor. They also made fun of the fact that he was Jewish and rather overweight.

When the boys saw me coming, I'm sure they thought I viewed myself as Robin Hood II, protector of the innocent and friend of the oppressed. One of the young tormentors ran straight up to my face and stared defiantly in my eyes. He was about half my size, but obviously felt safe because he was a teenager. He said, "You just hit me! I'll sue you for everything you're worth!"

I have rather large hands to go with my six-foot-two, 195-pound frame. It was obviously time to use them. I grasped his shoulder muscles on both sides, squeezing firmly. He immediately dropped to the ground, holding his neck. He rolled away and ran off with his friends, screaming insults back at me.

I reported the incident and later that evening received a phone call from the police. I was told the four young thugs had been harassing merchants and customers along that block for weeks. Their parents refused to cooperate with authorities, and the police felt hamstrung. Without the parents' help, they didn't know what to do. As I reflect now on that incident, I can think of no better way to breed and cultivate juvenile delinquency than for society to allow such early defiance to succeed with impunity. Leonardo da Vinci is quoted as saying, "He who does not punish evil commands it to be done."

Discipline outside the home is not very different from discipline inside. The principles by which children can be controlled are the same in both settings—only the application changes. A teacher, scoutmaster, or recreation leader who tries to control a group of children with anger is due for incredible frustration. The children will discover how far the adult will go before taking any action, and they invariably push him or her right to that line.

It is surprising to observe how often a teacher or group leader will impose disciplinary measures that children do *not* dislike. I knew a teacher, for example, who would scream and threaten and beg her class to cooperate. When they got completely out of hand, she would climb atop her desk and blow a whistle! The kids loved it! She weighed about two hundred and forty pounds, and the children would plot during lunch and recess about how they could get her atop that desk. She was inadvertently offering entertainment—a reward for their unruliness. It was much more fun than studying multiplication tables! Their attitude was much like that of Brer Rabbit, who begged the fox not to throw him in the briar patch. There was nothing they wanted more.

One should never underestimate a child's awareness that he is breaking the rules. I think most children are rather analytical about defying adult authority: they consider the deed in advance and weigh its probable consequences. If the odds are too great that justice will triumph, they'll take a safer course. This observation is verified in millions of homes where a youngster will push one parent to the limit of tolerance, but remain a sweet angel with the other. Mom whimpers, "Rick minds his dad perfectly, but pays no attention to me." Rick is no dummy. He knows Mom is safer than Dad.

To summarize this point, the parent must recognize that the most successful techniques of control are those which manipulate something of importance to the child. Yakkity-yak discussions and empty threats carry little or no motivational power for the child. "Why don't you straighten up and do what's right, Jack? What am I going to do with you, son? Mercy me, it seems like I'm always having to get on you. I just can't see why you don't do what you're told. If one time, just one time, you would act your age." On and on goes the barrage of words.

Jack endures the endless tirades, month in, month out, year after year. Fortunately for him, he is equipped with a mechanism that allows him to hear what he *wants* to hear and screen out everything else. Just as a person living by railroad tracks eventually does not even hear the trains rumbling by, so Jack has learned to ignore meaningless noise in his environment. Jack (and all his contemporaries) would be much more willing to cooperate if it were clearly to his personal advantage.

4. *Don't saturate the child with materialism.* Despite the hardships of the Great Depression, at least one question was then easier to answer than it is today: how can I say no to my child's materialistic desires? It was very simple for parents to tell their children that they couldn't afford to buy them everything they wanted; Dad could barely keep bread on the table. But in more opulent times, the parental task becomes less believable. It takes considerably more courage to say, "No, I *won't* buy you Wanda Wee-Wee and Baby-Blow-Her-Nose," than it did to say, "I'm sorry but you know we can't afford to buy those dolls."

A child's demand for expensive toys is carefully generated through millions of dollars spent on TV advertising by the manufacturers. The commercials are skillfully made so that the toys look like full-sized copies of their real counterparts; jet airplanes, robot monsters, and automatic rifles. The little consumer sits openmouthed in utter fascination. Five minutes later he begins a campaign that will eventually cost his dad $84.95 plus batteries and tax.

The trouble is, Dad often *can* afford to buy the new item, if not with cash, at least with his magic credit card. And when three other children on the block get the coveted toys, Mom and Dad begin to feel the pressure, and even the guilt. They feel selfish because they have indulged themselves for similar luxuries. Suppose the parents are courageous enough to resist the child's urging; he is not blocked—grandparents are notoriously easy to "con." Even if the youngster is unsuccessful in getting his parents or grandparents to buy what he wants, there is an annual, foolproof resource: Santa Claus! When junior asks Santa to bring him something, his parents are in an inescapable trap. What can they say, "Santa can't afford it"? Is the jolly fat man in the red suit really going to forget and disappoint him? No, the toy will be on Santa's sleigh.

Some would ask, "And why not? Why shouldn't we let our children enjoy the fruits of our good times?" Certainly I would not deny boys and girls a reasonable quantity of the things they crave. But many American children are inundated with excesses that work toward their detriment. It has been said that prosperity offers a greater test of character than does adversity, and I'm inclined to agree.

There are few conditions that inhibit a sense of appreciation more than for a child to feel he is entitled to whatever he wants, whenever he wants it. It is enlightening to watch as a boy or girl tears open stacks of presents at a birthday party or perhaps at Christmas time. One after another, the expensive contents are tossed aside with little more than a glance. The child's mother is made uneasy by his lack of enthusiasm and appreciation, so she says, "Oh Marvin! Look what it is. It's a little tape recorder! What do you say to Grandmother? Give Grandmother a big hug. Did you hear me, Marvin? Go give Grams a big hug and kiss."

Marvin may or may not choose to make the proper noises to Grandmother. His lack of exuberance results from the fact that prizes which are won cheaply are of little value, regardless of the cost to the original purchaser.

There is another reason that the child should be denied some of the things he thinks he wants. Although it sounds paradoxical, you actually cheat him of pleasure when you give him too much. A classic example of this saturation principle is evident in my household each year during the Thanksgiving season. Our family is blessed with several of the greatest cooks who ever ruled a kitchen, and several times a year they do their "thing." The traditional Thanksgiving dinner consists of turkey, dressing, cranberries, mashed potatoes, sweet potatoes, peas, hot rolls, two kinds of salads, and six or eight other dishes.

Prior to my heart attack in 1990, I joined my family in a disgraceful but wonderful gastronomic ritual during the holiday season. We all ate until we were uncomfortable, not saving room for dessert. Then the apple pie, pound cake, and fresh ambrosia were brought to the table. It just didn't seem possible that we could eat another bite, yet somehow we did. Finally, taut family members began to stagger away from their plates, looking for a place to fall.

Later, about three o'clock in the afternoon, the internal pressure began to subside and someone passed the candy around. As the usual time for the evening meal arrived, no one was hungry, yet we had come to expect three meals a day. Turkey and roll sandwiches were constructed and consumed, followed by another helping of pie. By this time, everyone is a bit blank-eyed, absent-mindedly eating what they neither wanted nor enjoyed. This ridiculous ritual continued for two or three days, until the thought of food became rather disgusting. Whereas eating ordinarily offers one of life's greatest pleasures, it loses its thrill when the appetite for food is satisfied.

There is a broader principle to be considered here. Pleasure occurs when an intense need is satisfied. If there is no need, there is no pleasure. A simple glass of water is worth more than gold to a man dying of thirst. The analogy to children should be obvious. If you never allow a child to want something, he never enjoys the pleasure of receiving it. If you buy him a tricycle before he can walk, a bicycle before he can ride, a car before he can drive, and a diamond ring before he knows the value of money, he accepts these gifts with little pleasure and less appreciation. How unfortunate that such a child never had the chance to long for something, dreaming about it at night and plotting for it by day. He might have even gotten desperate enough to work for it. The same possession that brought a yawn could have been a trophy and a treasure. I suggest that you show your child the thrill of temporary deprivation; it's more fun and much less expensive.

Before leaving this thought, let me share a relevant illustration from the closing days of my father's life. He had suffered a massive heart attack, which placed his future in jeopardy. As he contemplated his own passing, he became even more fascinated with life. Everything in God's creation interested him, from science to the arts. He even developed a personal knowledge of and a friendship with the birds that gathered around his house. He named them all and had many eating out of his hand. That is what led to . . . the starling incident.

For some reason, a mother bird abandoned her four baby starlings before they were able to fend for themselves. That precipitated an intense effort in the Dobson household to save the starlings by all means possible. Admittedly, they belonged to a despised, disease-ridden species, but my father was a sucker for *anything* in real need. Thus, a rescue effort was launched. A couple of weeks later, I received the following letter from my mother, describing what had happened to their feathered little friends.

> Dear Family: If I could write like you, Jim, I'd make the last eleven days come alive as your dad and I lived them in a bird world. As you know, the four surviving starlings, Eenie, Meenie, Minie and Moe, were evicted from their "under the shingle" nest, and we adopted them. Their feathers were down like fuzz and their bod-

ies seemed to consist of legs, wings, and mouths. They chirped constantly to be fed, after which their cries settled into a lovely lullaby. They outgrew their first cozy nest and your dad transferred them to a larger box from which they could not escape. So the only exposure they had to the outside world was the 2' x 3' area above their heads. They seemed to know this opening was where the action was, so they huddled together with their heads turned upward, tweet-tweeting their little tunes. When your dad peered over the top with our dog, Benji, all four birds would open their yellow beaks—chirping—"Worms! Worms!"

As the foursome grew, they sat on a tree limb where your dad placed them. Sometime jumping to the ground, they followed him around the yard, cuddling his shoes and not letting him get more than a few inches away. Their jerky movements made it impossible to keep pace.

From the beginning, we were unsure what we should feed them. Your dad gave them soft bread and milk—dipping it with tweezers into their wide open beaks . . . along with worms, grain, and a few drops of water from an eyedropper. However, on the ninth morning, Jimmy found Moe dead. What to do?! The tenth afternoon Meenie died. The eleventh night he looked down at the two remaining birds. Even while he looked at them, Minie gave a long "Chirp," lay down, stretched out his legs, and died. That left Eenie, the strongest of the birds . . . the one with the most vitality and personality. This morning, however, his vocalizations were desperate and weaker. He only lived until noon. As Jimmy bent over the box nest, Eenie recognized his presence, reached toward him and gave one last "cheep," and was gone.

How sad we both were—that we somehow had failed the helpless creatures who tried so hard to live and fly in the beautiful sky. Your father's love for those insignificant birds and his sadness over their loss reveal the soul of the man I married and have lived with for forty-three years. Does anyone wonder why I love this man?

Your Mother

The man who was so loved by my mother was not long for this world. He died a month later while sitting at the dinner table. His last act before falling into her arms was to express a prayer of blessing on the meal he would not live to eat.

And the starlings? The best explanation for their failure to thrive is that my dad simply overfed them. He was fooled by their constant plea for food. In an effort to satisfy their need, my father actually killed the birds he sought desperately to save.

Does the point come through? We parents too, in our great love for our children, can do irreparable harm by yielding to their pleas for more and more things. There are times when the very best reply we can offer is . . . no.

5. *Establish a balance between love and discipline.* We come now to the foundational understanding on which the entire parent-child relationship rests. It is to be found in a careful balance between love and discipline. The interaction of those two variables is critical and is as close as we can get to a formula for successful parenting.

We've already looked at the first factor, disciplinary control, and what the extremes of oppression and permissiveness do to a child. The other ingredient, parental love, is equally vital. In homes where children are not adored by at least one parent (or a parent-figure), they wither like a plant without water.

It has been known for decades that an infant who is not loved, touched, and caressed will often die of a strange disease initially called marasmus. They simply wither up and die before their first birthday. Evidence of this emotional need was observed in the thirteenth century, when Frederick II conducted an experiment with fifty infants. He wanted to see what language they would speak if they never had the opportunity to hear the spoken word. To carry out this dubious research project, he assigned foster mothers to bathe and suckle the children, but forbade them to fondle, pet, or talk to their charges. The experiment failed dramatically because all fifty infants died. Hundreds of more recent studies indicate that the mother-child relationship during the first year of life is apparently vital to the infant's survival. An unloved child is truly the saddest phenomenon in all of nature.

While the absence of love has a predictable effect on children, it is not so well known that excessive love or "super love" imposes its hazards, too. I believe some children are spoiled by love, or what passes for love. Some Americans are tremendously child-oriented at this stage in their history; they have invested all of their hopes, dreams, desires, and ambitions in their youngsters. The natural culmination of this philosophy is overprotection of the next generation.

I dealt with one anxious parent who stated that her children were the only source of satisfaction in living. During the long summers, she spent most of her time sitting at the front room window, watching her three girls while they played. She feared that they might get hurt or need her assistance, or they might ride their bikes in the street. Her other responsibilities to her family were sacrificed, despite her husband's vigorous complaints. She did not have time to cook or clean her house; guard duty at the window was her only function. She suffered enormous tensions over the known and unknown dangers that could threaten her beloved offspring.

Childhood illness and sudden danger are always difficult for a loving parent to tolerate, but the slightest threat produces unbearable anxiety for the overprotective mom and dad. Unfortunately, the parent is not the only one who suffers; the child is often its victim, too. He or she is not permitted to take reasonable risks—risks which are a necessary prelude to growth and development. Likewise, the materialistic problems described in the previous section are often maximized in a family where the children can be denied nothing. Prolonged emotional immaturity is another frequent consequence of overprotection.

I should mention another unfortunate circumstance, which occurs too often in our society. It is present in homes where the mother and father represent opposing extremes in control. The situation usually follows a familiar pattern: Dad is a very busy man, and he is heavily involved in his work. He is gone from early morning to night, and when he does return, he brings home a briefcase full of work. Perhaps he travels frequently. During the rare times when he is home and not working, he is exhausted. He collapses in front of the TV set to watch a ball game, and he doesn't want to be bothered. Consequently, his approach to child management is harsh and unsympathetic. His temper flares regularly, and the children learn to stay out of his way.

By contrast, Mom is much more supportive. Her home and her children are her sources of joy; in fact, they have replaced the romantic fires which have vanished from her marriage. She worries about Dad's lack of affection and tenderness for the children. She feels that she should compensate for his sternness by leaning in the other direction. When he sends the children to bed without their supper, she slips them some milk and cookies. Since she is the only authority on the scene when Dad is gone, the predominant tone in the home is one of unstructured permissiveness. She needs the children too much to risk trying to control them.

Thus, the two parental symbols of authority act to contradict each other, and the child is caught somewhere between them. The child respects neither parent because each has assassinated the authority of the other. It has been my observation that these self-destructing forms of authority often load a time bomb of rebellion that discharges during adolescence. The most hostile, aggressive teenagers I have known have emerged from this antithetical combination.

Again, The "middle ground" of love and control must be sought if we are to produce healthy, responsible children.

SUMMARY

Lest I be misunderstood, I shall emphasize my message by stating its opposite. I am not recommending that your home be harsh and oppressive. I am not suggesting that you give your children a spanking every morning with their ham and eggs, or that you make your boys sit in the living room with their hands folded and their legs crossed. I am not proposing that you try to make adults out of your kids so you can impress your adult friends with your parental skill, or that you punish your children whimsically, swinging and screaming when they didn't know they were wrong. I am not suggesting that you insulate your dignity and authority by being cold and unapproachable. These parental tactics do not produce healthy, responsible children. By contrast, I am recommending a simple principle: when you are defiantly challenged, win decisively. When the child asks, "Who's in charge?" tell him. When he mutters, "Who loves me?" take him in your arms and surround him with affection. Treat him with respect and dignity, and expect the same from him. Then begin to enjoy the sweet benefits of competent parenthood.

FOUR

Questions
and Answers

The discipline of children has become such a controversial and emotional issue, especially in the light of today's plague of child abuse, that the likelihood of misunderstanding is great in a book of this nature. To help clarify the philosophy from which I write, I have included the following questions and answers which were drawn from actual interactions with parents. Perhaps these items will put flesh on the bones of the structure I have built.

Q *You spoke of parents having a plan—a conscious goal in their approach to parenting. Would you apply that to preschoolers? What, specifically, should we be hoping to accomplish between eighteen months and five years of age?*

A There are two messages that you want to convey to preschoolers, and even those up through elementary school age. They are (1) "I love you, little one, more than you can possibly understand. You are precious to your (father) and me, and I thank God that he let me be your (mother)" and (2) "Because I love you so much, I must teach you to obey me. That is the only way I can take care of you and protect you from things that might hurt you."[1] Let's read what the Bible says to us: "Children, obey your parents in the Lord, for this is right." (Eph. 6:1, NIV). This is an abbreviated answer to a very important and complex question, but perhaps it will give you a place to begin formulating your own philosophy of parenting.

Q *We hear so much about the importance of communication between a parent and child. If you suppress a child's defiant behavior, how can he express the hostility and resentment he feels?*

A The child should be free to say *anything* to his parent, including "I don't like you" or "You weren't fair with me, Mommy." These expressions of true feeling should not be suppressed, provided they are said in a respectful manner. There is a thin line between what is acceptable and unacceptable behavior at this point. The child's expression of strong feeling, even resentment and anger, should be encouraged if it exists. But the parent should prohibit the child from resorting to name-calling and open rebellion. "Daddy, you hurt my feelings in front of my friend, and you were unkind to me" is an acceptable statement. "You stupid idiot, why didn't you shut up when my friends were here?!" is obviously unacceptable. If approached rationally as depicted in the first statement, it would be wise for the father to sit down and try to understand the child's viewpoint. Dad should be big enough to apologize to the child if he feels he was wrong. If he was right, however, he should calmly explain why he reacted as he did and tell the child how they can avoid the collision next time. It is possible to communicate without sacrificing parental respect, and the child should be taught how to express his discontent properly. This will be a very useful communicative tool later in life.

Q *We have an adopted child who came to us when he was two years old. He lived in fear, however, during those first couple of years, and we feel sorry for him. That's why my husband and I cannot let ourselves punish him, even when he deserves it. We also feel we don't have the right to discipline him, since we are not his biological parents. Are we doing right?*

A I'm afraid you are making a mistake commonly committed by the parents of older adopted children. They pity their youngsters too much to confront them. They feel that life has already been too hard on the little ones and believe they must not make things worse by disciplining them. As you indicated, there is often the feeling that they do not have the right to make demands on their adopted children.

These guilt-laden attitudes can lead to unfortunate consequences. Transplanted children have the same needs for guidance and discipline as those remaining with their biological parents. One of the surest ways to make a child feel insecure is to treat him as though he is different, unusual, or brittle. If the parents view him as an unfortunate waif to be shielded, he will see himself that way, too.

Parents of sick and deformed children are also likely to find discipline harder to implement. A child with a withered arm or some nonfatal illness can become a little terror, simply because the usual behavioral boundaries are not established by the parents. It must be remembered that the need to be led and governed is almost universal in childhood. This need is not eliminated by other problems and difficulties in life. In some cases, the desire for boundaries is maximized by other troubles, for it is through loving control that parents express personal worth to a child.

Let me make one further comment about adopted children that should be noted. I would have answered the question differently if the adopted child had been physically abused. In cases where beatings and/or other harm occurred before the permanent home was found, it would be unwise to use corporal punishment. The memory of the early horror would likely make it difficult for a child to understand the corrective nature of the punishment. Other forms of discipline and great expressions of love are then in order for an abused child.

Q *Do you think a child should be required to say "thank you" and "please" around the house?*

A I sure do. Requiring those phrases is one method of reminding the child that this is not a "gimme-gimme" world. Even though parents cook for their children, buy for them, and give to them, the youngsters must assume a few attitudinal responsibilities in return. As I have already indicated, appreciation must be taught, and this instructional process begins with fundamental politeness.

Q *My husband and I are divorced, so I have to handle all the discipline of the children myself. How does this change the recommendations you've made?*

A Not at all. The principles of good discipline remain the same, regardless of the family setting. The procedures do become more difficult for one parent, like yourself, to implement, since you have no one to support you when the children become defiant. You have to play the role of the father *and* mother, which is not easily done. Nevertheless, children do not make allowances for your handicap. You must earn their respect, or you will not receive it.

Q *You have discussed the need for establishing boundaries within the home. Do children really want limits set on their behavior?*

A Most certainly! After working with and around children all these years, I could not be more convinced of this fact. They derive security from knowing where the boundaries are and who's available to enforce them. Perhaps an illustration will make this more clear. Imagine yourself driving a car over the Royal Gorge in Colorado. The bridge is suspended hundreds of feet above the canyon floor, and as a first-time traveler you are uneasy as you cross. (I knew one little fellow who was so awed by the view from the bridge that he said, "Wow, Daddy. If you fell off here it'd kill you constantly!") Now suppose there were no guardrails on the side of the bridge; where would you steer the car? Right down the middle of the road! Even though you wouldn't plan to hit the protective rails along the side, you'd feel more secure just knowing they were there.

The analogy to children has been demonstrated empirically. During the early days of the progressive education movement, one enthusiastic theorist removed the chain-link fence surrounding the nursery school yard. He thought children would feel more freedom of movement without the visible barrier surrounding them. When the fence was removed, however, the boys and girls huddled near the center of the playground. Not only did they not wander away, they didn't even venture to the edge of the grounds.

There is security in defined limits. When the home atmosphere is as it should be, children live in utter safety. They never get in trouble unless they deliberately ask for it, and as long as they stay within the limits, there is happiness and freedom and acceptance. If this is what is meant by "democracy" in the home, then I favor it. If it means the absence of boundaries, or that children set their own boundaries in defiance of parents, then I'm unalterably opposed to it.

Q *Permissiveness is a relative term. Please describe its meaning to you.*

A When I use the term permissiveness, I refer to the absence of effective parental authority, resulting in the lack of boundaries for the child. This word represents tolerance of childish disrespect, defiance, and the general confusion that occurs in the absence of adult leadership.

Q *I have never spanked my three-year-old because I am afraid it will teach her to hit others and be a violent person. Do you think I am wrong?*

A You have asked a vitally important question that reflects a common misunderstanding about child management. First, let me emphasize that it *is* possible . . . even easy . . . to create a violent and aggressive child who has observed this behavior at home. If he is routinely beaten by hostile, volatile parents, or if he witnesses physical violence between angry adults, or if he feels unloved and unappreciated within his family, the child will not fail to notice how the game is played. Thus, corporal punishment that is not administered according to very carefully thought-out guidelines is a dangerous thing. Being a parent carries *no* right to slap and intimidate a child because you had a bad day or are in a lousy mood. It is this kind of unjust discipline that causes some well-meaning authorities to reject corporal punishment altogether.

Just because a technique is used wrongly, however, is no reason to reject it altogether. Many children desperately need this resolution to their disobedience. In those situations when the child fully understands what he is being asked to do or not to do but refuses to yield to adult leadership, an appropriate spanking is the shortest and most effective route to an attitude adjustment. When he lowers his head, clenches his fists, and makes it clear he is going for broke, justice must speak swiftly and eloquently. Not only does this response not create aggression in a boy or girl, it helps them control their impulses and live in harmony with various forms of benevolent authority throughout life. Why? Because it is in harmony with nature, itself. Consider the purpose of minor pain in a child's life.

Suppose two-year-old Peter pulls on a tablecloth and a vase of roses on which it rests tips over the edge of the table, cracking him between the eyes. From this pain, he learns that it is dangerous to pull on the tablecloth unless he knows what sits on it. When he touches a hot stove, he quickly learns that heat must be respected. If he lives to be a hundred, he will never again reach out and touch the red-hot coils of a stove. The same lesson is learned when he pulls the doggy's tail and promptly receives a neat row of teeth marks across the back of his hand, or when he climbs out of his high chair when Mom isn't looking and discovers all about gravity.

For three or four years, he accumulates bumps, bruises, scratches, and burns, each one teaching him about life's boundaries. Do these experiences make him a violent person? No! The pain associated with these events teaches him to avoid making the same mistakes again. God created this mechanism as a valuable vehicle for instruction.

Now when a parent administers a reasonable spanking in response to willful disobedience, a similar nonverbal message is being given to the child. He must understand that there are not only dangers in the physical world to be avoided. He should also be wary of dangers in his social world, such as defiance, sassiness, selfishness, temper tantrums, behavior that puts his life in danger, etc. The minor pain that is associated with this deliberate misbehavior tends to inhibit it, just as discomfort works to shape behavior in the physical world.

Neither conveys hatred. Neither results in rejection. Neither makes the child more violent.

In fact, children who have experienced corporal punishment from loving parents do not have trouble understanding its meaning. I recall my good friends, Art and Ginger Shingler, who had four beautiful children whom I loved. One of them went through a testy period where he was just "asking for it." The conflict came to a head in a restaurant, when the boy continued doing everything he could to be bratty. Finally, Art took him to the parking lot for an overdue spanking. A woman passerby observed the event and became irate. She chided the father for "abusing" his son and said she intended to call the police. With that, the child stopped crying and said to his father, "What's wrong with that woman, Dad?" *He* understood the discipline even if his rescuer did not. A boy or girl who knows love abounds at home will not resent a well-deserved spanking. One who is unloved or ignored will hate *any* form of discipline!

Q *Do you think you should spank a child for every act of disobedience or defiance?*

A No. Corporal punishment should be a rather infrequent occurrence. There is an appropriate time for a child to sit on a chair to "think" about his misbehavior, or he might be deprived of a privilege, or sent to his room for a "time out," or made to work when he had planned to play. In other words, you should vary your response to misbehavior, always hoping to stay one step ahead of the child. Your goal is to react continually in the way that benefits the child, and in accordance with his "crime." In this regard, there is no substitute for wisdom and tact in the parenting role.

Q *Where would you administer a spanking?*

A It should be confined to the buttocks area, where permanent damage is very unlikely. I do not believe in slapping a child on the face, or in jerking him around by the arms. A common form of injury seen in the emergency room at Children's Hospital when I was there involved children with shoulder separations. Parents had pulled tiny arms angrily and dislocated the shoulder or elbow. If you spank a child only on the "behind" or on the upper part of the legs, I think you will be doing it right.

Q *Is there anyone who should never spank a child?*

A No one who has a history of child abuse should risk getting carried away again. No one who secretly "enjoys" the administration of corporal punishment should be the one to implement them. No one who feels himself or herself out of control should carry through with *any* physical response. And grandparents probably should not spank their grandkids *unless* the parents have given them permission to do so.

Q *Do you think corporal punishment will eventually be outlawed?*

A It is very likely. The tragedy of child abuse has made it difficult for people to understand the difference between viciousness to kids and constructive, positive forms of physical punishment. There are those in the Western world who will not rest until the government interferes with parent-child relationships with all the force of law. It has already happened in Sweden, and the media seems determined to bring that legislation to the United States. It will be a sad day for families. Child abuse will increase, not decrease, as frustrated parents explode after having no appropriate response to defiant behavior.

Q *There is some controversy over whether a parent should spank with his or her hand or with some other object, such as a belt or paddle. What do you recommend?*

A I recommend a neutral object of some type. To those who disagree on this point, I'd encourage them to do what seems right to them. It is not a critical issue to me. The reason I suggest a switch or paddle is because the hand should be seen as an object of love—to hold, hug, pat and caress. However, if you're used to suddenly disciplining with the hand, your child may not know when he's about to be swatted and can develop a pattern of flinching when you suddenly scratch your head. This is not a problem if you take the time to get a neutral object.

My mother always used a small switch, which *could not* do any permanent damage. But it stung enough to send a very clear message. One day when I had pushed her to the limit, she actually sent me to the backyard to cut my own instrument of punishment. I brought back a tiny little twig about seven inches long. She could not have generated anything more than a tickle with it. Thereafter, she never sent me on that fool's errand again.

As I conceded above, some people (particularly those who are opposed to spanking in the first place) believe that the use of a neutral object in discipline is tantamount to child abuse. I understand their concern, especially in cases when a parent believes "might makes right" or loses his temper and harms the child. That is why adults must always maintain a balance between love and control, regardless of the method by which they administer disciplinary action.

Q *Is there an age when you begin to spank? And at what age do you stop?*

A There is no excuse for spanking babies or children younger than fifteen to eighteen months of age. Even shaking an infant can cause brain damage and death at this delicate age! But midway through the second year (eighteen months), a boy or girl becomes capable of knowing what you're telling them to do or not do. They can then very gently be held responsible for how they behave. Suppose a child is reaching for an electric socket or something that will hurt him. You say, "No!" but he just looks at you and continues reaching toward it. You can see the smile of challenge on his face as he thinks, "I'm going to do it anyway!" I'd encourage you to thump his fingers just enough to sting. A small amount of pain goes a long way at that age and begins to introduce children to realities of the world and the importance of listening to what you say.

There is no magical time at the end of childhood when spanking becomes ineffective, because children vary so much emotionally and developmentally. But as a general guideline, I would suggest that *most* corporal punishment be finished prior to the first grade (six years old). It should taper off from there and stop when the child is between the ages of ten and twelve.

Q *If it is natural for a toddler to break all the rules, should he be disciplined for his defiance?*

A Many of the spankings and slaps given to toddlers could and should be avoided. They get in trouble most frequently because of their natural desire to touch, bite, taste, smell, and break everything within their grasp. However, this "reaching out" behavior is not aggressive. It is a valuable means for learning and should not be discouraged. I have seen parents slap their two-year-olds throughout the day for simply investigating their world. This squelching of normal curiosity is not fair to the youngster. It seems foolish to leave an expensive trinket where it will tempt him, and then scold him for taking the bait. If little fat-fingers insists on handling the china cups on the lower shelf, it is much wiser to distract him with something else than to discipline him for his persistence. Toddlers cannot resist the offer of a new plaything. They are amazingly easy to interest in less fragile toys, and parents should keep a few alternatives available for use when needed.

When, then, should the toddler be subjected to mild discipline? When he openly defies his parents' spoken commands! If he runs the other way when called, purposely slams his milk glass on the floor, dashes in the street when being told to stop, screams and throws a tantrum at bedtime, hits his friends—these are the forms of unacceptable behavior which should be discouraged. Even in these situations, however, all-out spankings are not often required to eliminate the behavior. A firm rap on the fingers or a few minutes sitting on a chair will convey the same message just as convincingly. Spankings should be reserved for a child's moments of greatest antagonism, usually occurring after the third birthday.

I feel it is important to stress the point made earlier. The toddler years are critical to a child's future attitude toward authority. He should be patiently taught to obey, without being expected to behave like a more mature child.

Without watering down anything I have said earlier, I should also point out that I am a firm believer in the judicious use of grace (and humor) in parent-child relationships. In a world in which children are often pushed to grow up too fast, too soon, their spirits can dry out like prunes beneath the constant gaze of critical eyes. It is refreshing to see parents temper their inclination for harshness with a measure of "unmerited favor." There is always room for more loving forgiveness within our homes. Likewise, there's nothing that rejuvenates the parched, delicate spirits of children faster than when a lighthearted spirit pervades the home and regular laughter fills its halls. Heard any good jokes lately?

Q *Sometimes my husband and I disagree on our discipline, and we will argue about what is best in front of our children. Do you think this is damaging?*

A Yes, I do. You and your husband should agree to go along with the decision of the other, at least in front of the child. The wisdom of the matter can be discussed later. When the two of you openly contradict each other, right and wrong begin to appear arbitrary to children.

Q *How do you feel about having a family council, where each member of the family has an equal vote on decisions affecting the entire family?*

A It's a good idea to let each member of the family know that the others value his viewpoint and opinion. Most important decisions should be shared within the group because that is an excellent way to build fidelity and family loyalty. However, the equal vote idea is carrying the concept too far. An eight-year-old should not have the same influence that his mother and father have in making decisions. It should be clear to everyone that the parents are the benevolent captains of the ship.

Q *My son obeys me at home, but is difficult to manage whenever I take him to a public place, like a restaurant. Then he embarrasses me in front of other people. Why is he like that? How can I change him?*

A Many parents do not like to punish or correct their children in public places where their disciplinary action is observed by critical onlookers. They'll enforce good behavior at home, but the child is "safe" when unfamiliar adults are around. In this situation, it is easy to see what the child has observed. He has learned that public facilities are a sanctuary where he can act any way he wishes. His parents are in a bind because of their self-imposed restriction. The remedy for this situation is simple: when little Roger decides to disobey in public, respond exactly as you would at home, except that Roger should be removed to a place where there is privacy. Or if he is older, you can promise to take up the matter as soon as you get home. Roger will quickly learn that the same rules apply everywhere, and that sanctuaries are not so safe after all.

Q *Should a child be disciplined for wetting the bed? How can you deal with this difficult problem?*

A Unless it occurs as an act or defiance after the child is awake, bed-wetting (enuresis) is an involuntary act for which he is not responsible. Disciplinary action under those circumstances is unforgivable and dangerous. He is humiliated by waking up wet, anyway, and the older he gets, the more foolish he feels about it. The bed wetter needs considerable reassurance and patience from parents, and they should try to conceal the problem from those who would laugh at him. Even good-natured humor within the family is painful when it is at the child's expense.

Bed-wetting has been the subject of much research, and there are several different causes in individual cases. In some children, the problem is physiological, resulting from a small bladder or other physical difficulty. A pediatrician or a urologist may be consulted in the diagnosis and treatment of such cases.

For others, the problem is unquestionably emotional in origin. Any change in the psychological environment of the home may produce midnight moisture. During summer camps conducted for young children, the directors often put plastic mattress covers on the beds of all the little visitors. The anxiety associated with being away from home apparently causes a high probability of bed-wetting during the first few nights, and it is particularly risky to be sleeping on the lower level of bunk beds! By the way, mattress covers are widely available and are a worthwhile investment for the home. They don't solve the problem, of course, but they do save in the "mopping up" effort afterward.

There is a third factor that I feel is the most frequent cause of enuresis, other than physical factors. During children's toddler years, they wet the bed because they simply have not mastered nighttime bladder control. Some parents then begin getting their children up at night routinely to go to the potty. There the youngster is still sound asleep, being told to "go tinkle" or whatever. Thus, as the toddler grows older and the need arises to urinate at night, he often dreams he is being told to turn loose. Even when partially awakened or disturbed at night, the child can believe he is being ushered to the bathroom. I would recommend that parents of older bed wetters stop getting them up at night, even if the bed-wetting continues for a while.

There are other remedies which sometimes work, such as electronic devices that ring a bell and awaken the child when the urine completes an electrical circuit. If the problem persists, a pediatrician or child psychologist can guide you in seeking a solution. In the meantime, it is important to help the child maintain self-respect despite his embarrassing trouble. And by all means, conceal your displeasure if it exists.

A sense of humor may help. I received a letter from a mother who wrote down her three-year-old son's bedtime prayer, "Now I lay me down to sleep. I close my eyes, I wet the bed."

Q *How long should a child be allowed to cry after being disciplined or spanked? Is there a limit?*

A Yes, I believe there should be a limit. As long as the tears represent a genuine release of emotion, they should be permitted to fall. But crying can quickly change from inner sobbing to an expression of protest aimed at punishing the enemy. Real crying usually lasts two minutes or less, but may continue for five. After that point, the child is merely complaining, and the change can be recognized in the tone and intensity of his voice. I would require him to stop the protest crying, usually by offering him a little more of whatever caused the original tears. In less antagonistic moments, the crying can easily be stopped by getting the child interested in something else.

Q *I have spanked my children for their disobedience and it didn't seem to help. Does this approach fail with some children?*

A Children are so tremendously variable that it is sometimes hard to believe they are all members of the same human family. Some boys and girls feel crushed from nothing more than a stern look, while others seem to require strong and even painful disciplinary measures to make a vivid impression. This difference usually results from the degree to which a child needs adult approval and acceptance. As I said earlier, the primary parental task is to get behind the eyes of the child, thereby tailoring the discipline to his unique perception.

In a direct answer to the question, it is generally not this individual variation that causes spanking to be ineffectual. When disciplinary measures fail, it is usually because of fundamental errors in their application. It is possible for twice the amount of punishment to yield half the results. I have made a study of situations where parents have told me their child ignores spankings and violates the same rule. There are five basic reasons for the lack of success.

1. *The most recurring problem results from infrequent, whimsical discipline.* Half the time the child is not disciplined for a particular act of defiance; the other half he is. Children need to know the certainty of justice. If there is a *chance* of beating the system, some will repeatedly try it.

2. *The child may be more strong-willed than the parent, and they both know it.* If he can outlast a temporary conflict, he has won a major battle, eliminating discipline as a tool in the parent's repertoire. The strongest of youngsters are tough enough to comprehend, intuitively, that the spanking *must not* be allowed to succeed. Thus, they stiffen their necks and gut it out. The solution is to outlast him and win, even if it takes a few rounds. The experience will be painful for both participants, but the benefits will come tomorrow and tomorrow and tomorrow.

3. *The parent suddenly employs a form of discipline after doing nothing for a year or two prior to that time.* It takes a child a while to respond to a new procedure, and parents might get discouraged during the adjustment period. But take heart in knowing that discipline will be effective over time if consistently applied.

4. *The spanking may be too gentle.* If it doesn't hurt it isn't worth avoiding next time. A slap with the hand on the bottom of a multi-diapered thirty-month old is not a deterrent to anything. While being careful not to go too far, you should ensure he feels the message.

5. *For a few children, this technique is simply not appropriate.* The neurologically handicapped child who is hyperactive, for example, may be made more wild and unmanageable by corporal punishment. The child who has been abused may identify loving discipline with the hatred of the past. And, the very sensitive child might need a different approach. Once more, there is no substitute for knowledge and understanding of a particular boy or girl.

Q *Should teenage children be spanked for disobedience or rudeness?*

A No! Teens desperately want to be thought of as adults, and they deeply resent being treated like children. Spanking is the ultimate insult at that age, and they are justified in hating it. Besides, it doesn't work. Discipline for adolescents and teens should involve lost privileges, financial deprivation, and related forms of non-physical retribution. Be creative!

My mother, I might note, was a master at trench warfare during my own stubborn adolescent years. My father was a full-time minister and frequently on the road, so Mom had the primary responsibility for raising me. I was giving my teachers a hard time during this era, and on several occasions was sent to the principal's office, where I received stern lectures and a few swats with an infamous rubber hose (which was permissible back then.) This discipline did not change my bad attitude, however, and my mother became increasingly frustrated with my irresponsibility and dropping grades. It wasn't long before she reached her limit.

One day after school she sat me down and said firmly, "I know you have been fooling around in school and ignoring your assignments. I also know you've been getting in trouble with your teachers." (She always seemed to have a team of detectives who told her every detail of my private life, although today I think it was little more than a keen mind, good eyes, and an unbelievable intuitive skill.) She continued, "Well, I've thought it over, and I've decided that I'm not going to do anything about what is going on. I'm not going to punish you. I'm not going to take away privileges. I'm not even going to talk about it anymore."

I was about to smile in relief when she said, "I do want you to understand one thing, however. If the principal ever calls *me* about your behavior, I promise you that the next day I'm going to school with you. I'm going to walk two feet behind you all day. I will hold your hand in front of all your friends in the hall and at lunch, and I'm going to enter into all your conversations throughout the whole day. When you sit in your seat, I'm going to pull my chair alongside you, or I'll even climb into the seat with you. For one full day, I will not be away from your side."

That promise absolutely terrified me. It would have been social suicide to have my "mommy" following me around in front of my friends. No punishment would have been worse! I'm sure my teachers wondered why there was such a sudden improvement in my behavior and a remarkable jump in my grades near the end of my freshman year in high school.

I simply couldn't run the risk of Mom getting that fatal phone call.

My mother knew that the threat of spanking is not the best source of motivation to a teenager. She had a better idea.

Q *My four-year-old frequently comes running home in tears because she has been hit by one of her little friends. I have taught her that it is not right to hit others, but now they are making life miserable for my little girl. What should I do?*

A I think you were wise to teach your daughter not to hit and hurt others, but self-defense is another matter. Children can be unmerciful to a defenseless child. When youngsters play together, they each want to have the best toys and determine the ground rules to their own advantage. If they find they can predominate by simply flinging a well-aimed fist at the nose of their playmate, someone is likely to get hurt. I'm sure there are those who disagree with me on this issue, but I believe you should teach your child to fight back when attacked.

I recently consulted with a mother who was worried about her small daughter's inability to defend herself. There was one child in their neighborhood who would crack three-year-old Ann in the face at the slightest provocation. This little bully, named Joan, was very small and feminine, but she never felt the sting of retaliation because Ann had been taught not to fight. I recommended that Ann's mother tell her to hit Joan back if she was hit first. Several days later the mother heard a loud altercation outside, followed by a brief scuffle. Then Joan began crying and went home. Ann walked casually into the house with her hands in her pockets, and explained, "Joan socked me so I had to help her remember not to hit me again." Ann had efficiently returned an eye for an eye and a tooth for a tooth. She and Joan have played together much more peacefully since that time.

Generally speaking, a parent should emphasize the stupidity of fighting. But to force a child to stand passively while being clobbered is to leave him at the mercy of his cold-blooded peers

Q *Look over your twenty-five years of dealing with parents and children. What is the very best disciplinary advice you can offer? What technique or method will help us manage our kids better than any other you've seen attempted?*

A My answer may not be what you expected, but it represents something I've observed frequently and know to be valid. The *best* way to get children to do what you want is to spend time with them before disciplinary problems occur—having fun together and enjoying mutual laughter and joy. When those moments of love and closeness happen, kids are not as tempted to challenge and test the limits. Many confrontations can be avoided by building friendships with kids and thereby making them *want* to cooperate at home. It sure beats anger as a motivator of little ones!

Q *I see now that I've been doing many things wrong with my children. Can I undo the harm?*

A Once the child reaches adolescence, it is very late to be reversing the trends; before that time, though, you may yet be able to instill the proper attitudes in your child. Fortunately we are permitted to make a few mistakes with our children. No one can expect to do everything right, and it is not the few errors that destroy a child. It is the consistent influence of conditions throughout childhood.

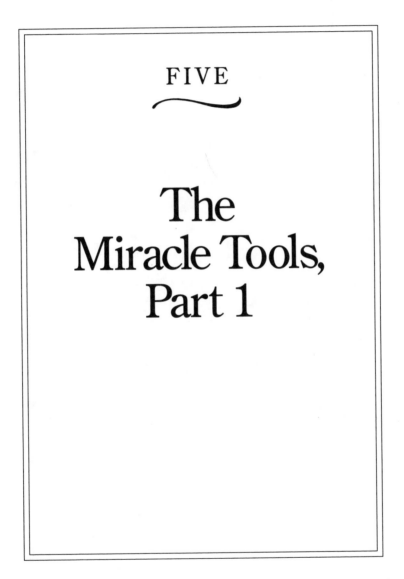

FIVE

The Miracle Tools, Part 1

I n the preceding chapters, we dealt with the proper parental response to a child's defiant "challenging behavior." Now we turn our attention to the leadership of children where antagonism is not involved. There are countless situations where the parent wishes to increase the child's level of responsibility, but that task is not easy. How can a mother get her child to brush his teeth regularly, or pick up his clothes, or display table manners? How can she teach him to be more responsible with money? What can the parent do to eliminate obnoxious habits, such as whining, sloppiness, or apparent laziness? Is there a solution to perpetual tardiness?

These kinds of behavior do not involve direct confrontations between parent and child, and should not be handled in the same decisive manner described previously. It would be unwise and unfair to punish a youngster for his understandable immaturity and childishness. A much more effective technique is available to use by the knowledgeable parent.

The first educational psychologist, E. L. Thorndike, developed an understanding of behavior in the 1920s that can be very useful for parents. He called it the "law of reinforcement." Later the concept became the basis for a branch of psychology known as behaviorism, which I resoundingly reject. Behaviorism was described by B. F. Skinner and J. B. Watson (mentioned earlier) and includes the unbelievable notion that the mind does not exist. One of my college textbooks referred to behaviorism as "psychology out of its mind." Well said! It perceives the human brain as a simple switchboard, connecting stimuli coming in with responses going out.

Despite my disagreement with the extrapolation of Thorndike's writings, there is no question that the original concept can be helpful to parents. Stated simply, the law of reinforcement reads, "Behavior which achieves desirable consequences will recur." In other words, if an individual likes what happens as a result of his behavior, he will be inclined to repeat that act. If Sally gets favorable attention from the boys on the day she wears a new dress, she will want to wear the dress again and again. If Pancho wins with one tennis racket and loses with another, he will prefer the racket with which he has found success. This principle is disarmingly simple, but it has interesting implications for human learning.

In the first edition of this book, I described the use of these techniques with our little dachshund, Sigmund Freud, (Siggy). Old Siggy lived for fifteen years, but has now gone on to wherever feisty dogs go when they die. It was fun training this stubborn animal by the use of reinforcement, which was the *only* thing that got his attention. Most dachshunds will sit up without being taught to do so, for example, because it is a natural response for the long-bodied animals to make. But not Siggy! He was unquestionably the world's most independent animal. During the first year of his life, I thought he was a little bit "slow" between the ears; the second year I began to think he might have been mentally deranged; eventually I came to see him as a recalcitrant, stubborn rascal who just wanted to do things his own way.

In short, it was difficult to entice Siggy to cooperate in any self-improvement programs without offering him an edible incentive. He was particularly fond of cookies, however, and I utilized this passion to good advantage. I propped him in a vertical position where he remained for only a second or two before falling. Then I gave him a piece of an old-fashioned, chocolate chip cookie. He loved it. I sat him up again, and I fed him the goodie as he was falling. Siggy bounced all around the room, trying to take the remaining cookies away from me—but there was only one way to continue the snack. Even Siggy began to get that idea.

In about thirty minutes of this ridiculous exercise, the dachshund received the message loud and clear. Once it hit him, he rarely had four feet on the ground at one time! Throughout the day, he could be found propped up on his haunches, asking for a bite of something—anything. Eventually, I was sorry I started the game, because I felt guilty ignoring him. After all, it was my idea in the first place, and I was compelled to find him something to eat in the kitchen.

This reinforcement technique was also useful in teaching Siggy to go chase a ball (a fantastic demonstration of animal intelligence). I threw the ball about ten feet out in front of us, then dragged Sig by the nape of the neck to where it lay. I opened his mouth, put the ball in place, and dragged him back to the starting place. An oatmeal cookie was waiting at the finish line. It was even easier to get his cooperation this time because he began to grasp the concept of working for a reward. That idea became firmly ingrained and Siggy became rather creative in applying it to his advantage. If the family happened to eat dinner from trays in order to watch the evening news on television, Siggy stationed himself in the exact spot where everyone's line of vision crossed on the way to the tube. There he sat, bobbing and weaving and begging for a bite.

More serious attempts have been made to teach sophisticated behavior to animals by the principles of reinforcement. The results have been remarkable. A pigeon was taught to examine radio parts moving by on a conveyor belt. The bird evaluated each component and knocked the defective ones off the track, for which he received a pellet of grain. He sat there all day long, concentrating on his work. As one might imagine, the labor unions took a dim view of this process; the pigeon did not demand coffee breaks or other fringe benefits, and his wages were disgracefully low. Other animals have been taught to perform virtually human feats by the careful application of rewards.

Let me hasten to acknowledge what some of my readers might be thinking at this point. There is an unbridgeable chasm between children and animals. What do these techniques have to do with kids? Just this: Human beings are also motivated by what pleases them, and that fact can be useful in teaching responsible behavior to boys and girls. However, it is not sufficient to dole out gifts and prizes in an unplanned manner. There are specific principles which must be followed if the law of reinforcement is to achieve its full potential. Let's consider the elements of this technique in detailed application to children.

1. *Rewards must be granted quickly.* If the maximum effectiveness is to be obtained from a reward, it should be offered shortly after the desirable behavior has occurred. Parents often make the mistake of offering long-range rewards to children, but their successes are few. It is usually unfruitful to offer nine-year-old Joey a car when he is sixteen if he'll work hard in school during the next seven years. Second- and third-grade elementary children are often promised a trip to grandma's house next summer in exchange for good behavior throughout the year. Their obedience is typically unaffected by this lure. It is unsatisfactory to offer Mary Lou a new doll for Christmas if she'll keep her room straight in July. Most children have neither the mental capacity nor the maturity to hold a long-range goal in mind day after day. Time moves slowly for them; consequently, the reinforce-

ment seems impossible to reach and uninteresting to contemplate.

For animals, a reward should be offered approximately two seconds after the behavior has occurred. A mouse will learn the turns in a maze much faster if the cheese is waiting at the end than he will when a five-second delay is imposed. Although children can tolerate longer delays than animals, the power of a reward is weakened with time.

Immediate reinforcement has been utilized successfully in the treatment of childhood autism, a major disorder which resembles childhood schizophrenia. The autistic child does not relate properly to his parents or any other people; he has no spoken language; he usually displays bizarre, uncontrollable behavior. What causes this distressing disorder? The evidence seems to point toward the existence of a biochemical malfunction in the autistic child's neural apparatus. For whatever cause, autism is extremely resistant to treatment.

How can a therapist help a child who can neither talk nor relate to him? All prior forms of treatment have been discouragingly ineffective, which led Dr. Ivar Lovaas and his colleagues to experiment many years ago with the use of rewards. At the University of California at Los Angeles, autistic children were placed on a program designed to encourage speech. At first, a bit of candy was placed into the child's mouth whenever he uttered a sound of any kind; his grunts, groans, and growls were rewarded similarly. The next step was to reward him for more specific vowel sounds. When an "o" sound was to be taught, candy was "paid" for all accidental noises in the proper direction. As the child progressed, he was finally required to pronounce the names of certain objects or people to achieve the reinforcement. Two-word phrases were then sought, followed by more complicated sentence structure. Some language was taught to these unfortunate children by this simple procedure.

The same technique has been employed simultaneously in teaching the autistic child to respond to the people around him. He was placed in a small dark box which had one sliding wooden window. The therapist sat on the outside of the box, facing the child who peered out the window. As long as the child looked at the therapist, the window remained open. However, when his mind wandered and he began gazing around, the panel fell, leaving him in the dark for a few seconds. Although no child with severe autism has been successfully transformed into a normal individual, the use of reinforcement therapy did bring some of these patients to a state of civilized behavior. The key to this success has been the immediate application of a pleasant consequence to desired behavior.

An understanding of how reinforcement works is not only useful in hospitals for autistic children. It also helps explain the way behavior works at home, as we have seen. For example, parents often complain about the irresponsibility of their youngsters, yet they fail to realize that some of this lack of industriousness has been learned. Most human behavior is learned—both the desirable and the undesirable responses. Children learn to laugh, play, run, and jump; they also learn to whine, bully, pout, fight, throw temper tantrums, or be tomboys. The unseen teacher is reinforcement. The child repeats the behavior which he considers to be successful. A youngster may be cooperative and helpful because he enjoys the effect that behavior has on his parents; another will sulk and pout for the same reason. When parents recognize characteristics which they dislike in their children, they should set about teaching more admirable traits by allowing good behavior to succeed and bad behavior to fail.

Described below are the steps of a program devised by Dr. Malcolm Williamson and myself when we were both serving on the attending staff at Children's Hospital of Los Angeles.

The system is useful with boys and girls between four and eight years of age; it can be modified in accordance with the age and maturity of the youngster.

    a. The chart on the next page lists some responsibilities and behaviors which the parent may wish to instill. These fourteen items constitute a much greater degree of cooperation and effort than most five-year-old children can display on a daily basis, but the proper use of rewards can make it seem more like fun than work. Immediate reinforcement is the key; each evening, colored dots (preferably red) or stars should be placed by the behaviors that were done satisfactorily. If dots are not available, the squares can be colored with a felt-tip pen; however, the child should be allowed to chalk up his own successes.

    b. Two pennies should be granted for every behavior done properly in a given day; if more than three items are missed in one day, no pennies should be given.

    c. Since a child can earn a maximum of twenty-eight cents a day, the parent has an excellent opportunity to teach him how to manage his money. It is suggested that he be allowed to spend only sixty to eighty cents per week of these earnings. Special trips to the store or toy shop can be planned. The daily ice cream truck used to provide a handy source of reinforcement, although an increasing number of parents today are trying to limit the fat and sugar their children eat. Of the remaining $1.16 to $1.36 (maximum), the child can be required to give twenty cents in the church offering or to some other charitable recipient; he should then save about thirty cents per week. The balance can be accumulated for a long-range expenditure for something he wants or needs.

"My Jobs"

November	14	15	16	17	18	19	20	21	22	23	24	25	26	27	28	29	30
1. I brushed my teeth without being told...............																	
2. I straightened my room before bedtime...............																	
3. I picked up my clothes without being told............																	
4. I fed the fish without being told																	
5. I emptied the trash without being told																	
6. I minded Mommy today																	
7. I minded Daddy today......................................																	
8. I said my prayers tonight																	
9. I was kind to little brother Billy today................																	
10. I took my vitamin pill.....................................																	
11. I said "thank you" and "please" today..............																	
12. I went to bed last night without complaining......																	
13. I gave clean water to the dog today..................																	
14. I washed my hands and came to the table when called																	
TOTAL:																	

d. The list of behaviors to be rewarded does not remain static. Once the child has gotten into the habit of hanging up his clothes, or feeding the puppy, or brushing his teeth, the parent should then substitute new responsibilities. A new chart should be made each month, and Junior can make suggestions for his revised chart.

This system provides several side benefits, in addition to the main objective of teaching responsible behavior. Through its use, for example, the child learns to count. He is taught to give to worthy causes. He begins to understand the concept of saving. He learns to restrict and control his emotional impulses. And finally, he is taught the meaning of money and how to spend it wisely. The advantages to his parents are equally impressive. A father of four young children applied the technique and later told me that the noise level in his household had been reduced noticeably.

Note: This plan is described almost exactly as it appeared in the original *Dare to Discipline*. Since then, I've heard many success stories and a few complaints. The most common negative comments have come from parents who said the task of keeping track of such a complex accounting system is burdensome every night. It takes fifteen or twenty minutes to put up the stars and measure out the pennies. If that is a concern in your family I would suggest that fewer goals be charted. Selecting even five important behaviors and rewarding them with three to five cents each would do the job just as well. *Make the system work for you*, modifying the concept as needed. I assure you, however, it *will* work if properly applied.

If this kind of reinforcement is so successful, why has it not been used more widely? Unfortunately, many adults are reluctant to utilize rewards because they view them as a source of bribery. One of our most successful teaching devices is ignored because of a philosophical misunderstanding. Our entire society is established on a system of reinforcement, yet we don't want to apply it where it is needed most: with young children. As adults, we go to work each day and receive a pay check on Friday. Is that bribery by the employer? Medals are given to brave soldiers; plaques are awarded to successful businessmen; watches are presented to retiring employees. Rewards make responsible effort worthwhile. That's the way the adult world works.

The main reason for the overwhelming success of capitalism is that hard work and personal discipline are rewarded in many ways. The great weakness of socialism is the absence of reinforcement; why should a man struggle to achieve if there is nothing special to be gained? This is, I believe, the primary reason communism failed miserably in the former Soviet Union and Eastern Europe. There was no incentive for creativity and "sweat equity."

I heard of a college chemistry course where the hardest working student in the class, Brains McGuffey, spent many long hours preparing for the first examination. The day of the test, he scored 90 points and earned a solid A. Another student, Ralph Ripoff, rarely ever cracked a book. He took the big exam without any preparation and earned a whopping 50 points for his effort. An "F" was recorded in the grade book.

However, the professor was a staunch believer in socialistic principles. He was disturbed that Brains had 20 points more than he really needed to pass, and Ralph was 20 points short. This didn't seem fair to the good doctor. Thus the points were redistributed and both students passed with a gentleman's "C." But . . . Brains never studied for another chemistry exam. Do you blame him?

Communism and Socialism are *destroyers* of motivation, because they penalize creativity and effort. They reward mediocrity and slovenliness. The law of reinforcement is violated by the very nature of those economic systems. Free enterprise works hand in hand with human nature.

Some parents implement a miniature system of socialism at home. Their children's wants and desires are provided by the "State," and are not linked to diligence or discipline in any way. However, they expect little Juan and René to carry responsibility simply because it is noble for them to do so. They want them to learn and sweat for the sheer joy of personal accomplishment. Most are not going to buy it.

Consider the alternative approach to the "bribery" I've recommended. How are you going to get your five-year-old to perform the behaviors listed on the chart? The most frequently used substitutes are nagging, complaining, begging, screaming, threatening, and punishing. The mother who objects to the use of rewards may also go to bed each evening with a headache, vowing to have no more children. She doesn't like to accentuate materialism in this manner, yet later she may *give* money to her child. Since her youngster never handles his own cash, he doesn't learn how to save it or spend it wisely. The toys she buys him are purchased with her money, and he values them less. But most important, he is not learning the self-discipline and personal responsibility that are possible through the careful reinforcement of that behavior.

Admittedly, there are tasks that a child should do because he is a member of the family. Washing the dishes or carrying out the trash may be expected and not reinforced. I agree that rewards should not be offered for every task done at home. But when you want your children to go above and beyond that base, such as cleaning the garage, or if you want to reinforce a better attitude, there is a more efficient approach then nagging and threatening!

Still, the concept remains controversial. I watched the application of these contrasting viewpoints in two actual home situations. Daren's parents were philosophically opposed to the reinforcement that they called bribes. Consequently, he was not rewarded (paid) for his efforts around the home. Daren hated his work because there was no personal gain involved in the effort; it was something to be tolerated.

When he had to mow the lawn on Saturday, he would drag himself out to the disaster area and gaze with unfocused eyes at the depressing task before him. As might be expected, he did a miserably poor job because he was absolutely devoid of motivation. This sloppiness bought a tongue-lashing from his dad, which hardly made the experience a pleasant one. Daren's parents were not stingy with him. They supplied his needs and even gave him some spending money. When the State Fair came to town, they would provide money for him to spend. Because their gifts were not linked to his responsible efforts, the money provided no source of motivation. Daren grew up hating to work; his parents had inadvertently reinforced his irresponsibility.

Brian's parents took a different view. They felt that he should be paid for the tasks that went beyond his regular household duties. He was not rewarded for carrying out the trash or straightening his room, but he received money for painting the fence on Saturday. This hourly wage was a respectable amount, comparable to what he *could* earn outside the family. Brian loved his work. He'd get up in the morning and attack the weeds in his backyard. He would count his money and work and look at his watch and work and count his money. At times he rushed home from school to get in an hour or two before dark. He opened his own bank account and was very careful about how he surrendered his hard-earned cash. Brian enjoyed great status in his neighborhood because he always had money in his pocket. He didn't spend it very often, but he could have done so at any given moment. That was power! At one point he drew all of his money out of the bank and asked for the total amount in new one dollar bills. He then stacked his twenty-eight bills in his top dresser drawer, and displayed them casually to Daren and his other penniless friends. Work and responsibility were the keys to this status, and he learned a good measure of both.

Brian's parents were careful never to give him a cent. They bought his clothes and necessities, but he purchased his own toys and personal indulgences. From an economic point of view, they spent no more money than did Daren's mom and dad; they merely linked each penny to the behavior they desired. I believe their approach was the more productive of the two.

As implied before, it is very important to know when to use rewards and when to resort to punishment. It is not recommended that rewards be utilized when the child has challenged the authority of the parent. For example, mom may say, "Pick up your toys, Lisa, because friends are coming over," and Lisa refuses to do so. It is a mistake for mom then to offer a piece of candy if Lisa will comply with her request. She would actually be rewarding her defiance.

If there is still confusion about how to respond in this kind of direct conflict, I suggest the reader take another look at chapters 1 to 4 of this book. Rewards should not be used as a substitute for authority; reward and punishment each has its place in child management, and reversals bring unfortunate results.

2. *Rewards need not be material in nature.* When my daughter was three years of age, I began to teach her some pre-reading skills, including the alphabet. In those days, I worried less about nutrition than I do now, and I often used bits of chocolate candy as my reinforcement. Late one afternoon I was sitting on the floor drilling Danae on several new letters when a tremendous crash shook the house. The whole family rushed outside to see what had happened and observed that

a teenager had wrecked his car in our quiet residential neighborhood. The boy was not badly hurt, but his automobile was upside-down in the street. We sprayed the smoldering car with water to keep the dripping gas from igniting and made the necessary phone call to the police. It was not until the excitement began to lessen that we realized our daughter had not followed us out of the house.

I returned to the den, where I found her elbow-deep in the two-pound bag of candy I had left behind. She had put at least a quarter-pound of chocolate into her mouth, and most of the remainder was distributed around her chin, nose, and forehead. When she saw me coming, she managed to jam another handful into her chipmunk cheeks. From this experience, I learned one of the limitations of using material, or at least edible, reinforcement.

Anything that is considered desirable to an individual can serve as reinforcement for his behavior. The most obvious rewards for animals are those which satisfy physical needs, although humans are further motivated to resolve their psychological needs. Some children, for example, would rather receive a sincere word of praise than a ten dollar bill, particularly if the adult approval is expressed in front of other children. Children and adults of all ages seek constant satisfaction of their emotional needs, including the desire for love, social acceptance, and self-respect. Additionally, they hope to find excitement, intellectual stimulation, entertainment, and pleasure.

Most children and adults are keenly interested in what their associates think and say. As a result, verbal reinforcement can be the strongest motivator of human behavior. Consider the tremendous impact of the following comments:

"Here comes Phil—the ugliest guy in school."

"Louise is so stupid! She never knows the right answer in class."

"Joe will strike out. He always does."

These unkind words burn like acid to the children they describe, causing them to modify future behavior. Phil may become quiet, withdrawn, and easily embarrassed. Louise will probably display even less interest in her schoolwork than before, appearing lazy to her teachers. Joe may give up baseball and other athletic endeavors.

It happened to me, in fact. I have always thought of myself as a "jock," playing various sports through the years. I lettered in college tennis all four years and captained the team when I was a senior. However, I never had much interest in baseball . . . and for good reason. When I was in the third grade, I stood in right field one day with the bases loaded. The entire third grade class . . . including many girls . . . had turned out to watch the big game, and everything was on the line. The batter slugged a routine fly ball in my direction, which inexplicably went through my fingers and straight to the ground. I picked up the ball in my embarrassment and threw it to the umpire. He stepped aside and let it roll for fifty yards. I can still hear the runner's feet pounding toward home plate. I can still hear the girls laughing. I can still feel my hot face out there in right field. I walked off the field that day and gave up a brilliant baseball career.

We adults are equally sensitive to the idle comments of our peers. It is often humorous to observe how vulnerable we are to the casual remarks of our friends (and even our enemies). "You've gained a few pounds, haven't you, Martha?" Martha may choose to ignore the comment for the moment, but she will spend fifteen minutes before the mirror that evening and start an diet program the next morning.

"Ralph is about your age, Pete; I'd say he is forty-six or forty-eight years old." Pete is only thirty-nine, and the blood drains from his face; the new concern over his appearance may be instrumental in his decision to purchase a hairpiece the following month. Our hearing apparatus is more attuned to this kind of personal evaluation than any other subject, and our sense of self-respect and worthiness emerge largely from these unintentional messages.

Verbal reinforcement should permeate the entire parent-child relationship. Too often our parental instruction consists of a million "don'ts" which are jammed down the child's throat. We should spend more time rewarding him for the behavior we desire, even if our "reward" is nothing more than a sincere compliment. Remembering the child's need for self-esteem and acceptance, the wise parents can satisfy those important longings while using them to teach valued concepts and behavior. A few examples may be helpful:

> Mother to daughter: "You certainly colored nicely within the lines on the picture, René. I like to see that kind of neat art work. I'm going to put this on the refrigerator."

> Mother to husband in son's presence: "Neil, did you notice how Don put his bicycle in the garage tonight? He used to leave it out until we told him to put it away; he is becoming much more responsible, don't you think?"

> Father to son: "I appreciate your being quiet while I was figuring the income tax, Son. You were very thoughtful. Now that I have that job done, I'll have more time. Why don't we plan to go to the zoo next Saturday?"

> Mother to small son: "Kevin, you haven't sucked your
> thumb all morning. I'm very proud of you. Let's see
> how long you can go this afternoon."

It is unwise for a parent to compliment the child for behavior she does not admire. If everything the child does earns him a big hug and a pat on the back, Mom's approval gradually becomes meaningless. Specific behavior warranting genuine compliments can be found if it is sought, even in the most mischievous youngster.

Well, let's pause for a few relevant questions and answers, and then return to the next chapter to some additional thoughts about the law of reinforcement.

QUESTIONS AND ANSWERS

Q *Can rewards be employed in a church or Sunday school program?*

A I have seen reinforcement utilized with great effectiveness in a Christian Sunday school. Instead of earning money, children accumulated "talents" which resemble toy money of various denominations. (The concept of talents was taken from Jesus' parable in Matthew 25:15.) The children earned talents by memorizing Scripture verses, being punctual on Sunday morning, having perfect attendance, bringing a visitor, and so on. This system of currency was then used to obtain new items from those on display in a glass case. Bibles, pens, books, puzzles, and other religious or educational prizes were available for selection.

The children's division blossomed in the church where this system was employed. However, some people may oppose this materialistic program in a church setting, and that is a matter for individual evaluation.

Q *Must I brag on my child all day for every little thing he does? Isn't it possible to create a spoiled brat by telling him his every move is wonderful?*

A Yes, inflationary praise is unwise. As I mentioned in an earlier book, Junior quickly catches on to your verbal game and your words then lose their meaning. It is helpful, therefore, to distinguish between the concepts of *flattery* and *praise.*

Flattery is unearned. It is what Grandma says when she comes for a visit: "Oh, look at my beautiful little girl! You're getting prettier each day. I'll bet you'll have to beat the boys off with a club when you get to be a teenager!" Or, "My, what a smart boy you are." Flattery occurs when you heap compliments upon the child for something he does not achieve.

Praise, on the other hand, is used to reinforce positive, constructive behavior. It should be highly specific rather than general. "You've been a good boy . . . " is unsatisfactory. "I like the way you kept your room clean today," is better. Parents should always watch for opportunities to offer genuine, well-deserved praise to their children, while avoiding empty flattery.[1]

Q *Should a parent try to force a child to eat?*

A No. In fact, the dinner table is one potential battlefield where a parent can easily get ambushed. You can't win there! A strong-willed child is like a good military general who constantly seeks an advantageous place to take on the enemy.

He need look no farther. Of all the common points of conflict between generations . . . bedtime, hair, clothes, schoolwork, etc., the advantages at the table are all in the child's favor! Three times a day, a very tiny child can simply refuse to open his mouth. No amount of coercing can make him eat what he doesn't want to eat.

I remember one three-year-old who was determined not to eat his green peas, and a father who had made up his mind the squishy little vegetables were going down. It was a classic confrontation between the irresistible force and an immoveable object. Neither would yield. After an hour of haranguing, threatening, cajoling and sweating, the father had not achieved his goal. The tearful toddler sat with a forkload of peas pointed ominously at his sealed lips.

Finally, through sheer intimidation, the dad managed to get one bite of peas in place. But the lad wouldn't swallow them. I don't know everything that went on afterwards, but the mother told me they had no choice but to put the child to bed with the peas still in his mouth. They were amazed at the strength of his will.

The next morning, the mother found a little pile of mushy peas where they had been expelled at the foot of the bed! Score one for Junior, none for Dad. Tell me in what other arena a thirty-five-pound child could whip a two-hundred-pound man?

Not every toddler is this tough, of course. But *many* of them will gladly do battle over food. It is their ideal power game. Talk to any experienced parent or grandparent and they will tell you this is true. The sad thing is that these conflicts are unnecessary. Children will eat as much as they need if you keep them from indulging in the wrong stuff. They will not starve. I promise!

The way to deal with a poor eater is to set good food before him. If he claims to not be hungry, wrap the plate, put it in the refrigerator and send him cheerfully on his way. He'll be back in a few hours. God has put a funny little feeling in his tummy that says, "gimme food!" When this occurs, *do not* put sweets, snacks or confectionery food in front of him. Simply retrieve the earlier meal, warm it up and serve it again. If he protests, send him out to play again. Even if twelve hours or more goes by, continue this procedure until food . . . all food . . . begins to look and smell wonderful. From that time forward, the battle over the dinner table should be history. (For a tape discussing this procedure, contact Focus on the Family, P.O. Box 35500, Colorado Springs, CO, 80935-3550, and ask for the interview entitled, "A Pediatrician's Advice on Discipline.")

Q *You stated earlier that you do not favor spanking teenagers. What would you do to encourage cooperation from my fourteen-year-old who deliberately makes a nuisance of himself? He throws his clothes around, refuses to help with any routine tasks in the house, and pesters his little brother to death. What am I to do about it?*

A The principles of reinforcement are particularly useful with teenagers, because such rewards appeal to youngsters during this typically self-centered time of life. However, laziness is an unavoidable fact of life with many adolescents. Their lack of industriousness and general apathy has a physiological origin. Their energy during early adolescence is being redirected into rapid growth. Also, glandular changes require a physical readjustment. For several years they may want to sleep until noon and drag themselves around until it comes time to do something that suits their fancy. If *any* system will succeed in charging their sluggish batteries, it will probably involve an incentive of some variety. The following three steps can be followed in implementing a system of reinforcement with a sixteen-year-old:

1. *Decide what is important to the youngster for use as an incentive.* Two hours with the family car on date night is worth the world to most newly licensed drivers. (This could be the most expensive incentive in history if the young driver is a bit shaky behind the wheel.) An allowance is another easily available source of motivation, as described above. Teenagers have a great need for cold cash today. A routine date with Helen Highschool might cost twenty dollars or more—in some cases *far* more. Yet another incentive may involve a fashionable article of clothing which would not ordinarily be within your teen's budget. Offering him or her a means of obtaining such luxuries is a happy alternative to the whining, crying, begging, complaining, and pestering that might occur otherwise. Mom says, "Sure you can have the ski sweater, but you'll have to earn it." Once an acceptable motivator is agreed upon, the second step can be implemented.

2. *Formalize the agreement.* A contract is an excellent means of settling on a common goal. Once an agreement has been written, it is signed by the parent and teen. The contract may include a point system which enables your teenager to meet the goal in a reasonable time period. If you can't agree on the point values, you could allow for binding arbitration from an outside party. Let's examine a sample agreement in which Marshall wants a compact disc player, but his birthday is ten months away and he's flat broke. The cost of the player is approximately $150. His father agrees to buy the device if Marshall earns 10,000 points over the next six to ten weeks doing various tasks. Many of these opportunities are outlined in advance, but the list can be lengthened as other possibilities become apparent:

  a. For making bed and straightening room
     each morning . . . . 50 points

b. For each hour of studying . . . . 150 points
c. For each hour of house or yard work done . 300 points
d. For being on time at breakfast and dinner . . 40 points
e. For babysitting siblings per hour . . . . . . 150 points
f. For washing car each week . . . . 250 points
g. For arising by 8:00 A.M. Saturday
   morning . . . . 100 points

While the principles are almost universally effective, the method of application must be varied. With a little imagination, you can create a list of chores and point values that work in your family. It's important to note that points can be gained for cooperation and lost for resistance. Disagreeable and unreasonable behavior can be penalized 50 points or more. (However, penalties must be imposed fairly and rarely or the entire system will crumble). Also, bonus points can be awarded for behavior that is particularly commendable.

3. *Establish a method to provide immediate rewards.* Remember that prompt reinforcement achieves the best results. This is necessary to sustain teens' interest as they move toward the ultimate goal. A thermometer-type chart can be constructed, with the point scale listed down the side. At the top is the 10,000-point mark, beside a picture of a compact disc player or other prize. Each evening, the daily points are totalled and the red portion of the thermometer is extended upward. Steady, short-term progress might earn Marshall a bonus of some sort—perhaps a CD of his favorite musician or a special privilege. If he changes his mind about what he wishes to buy, the points can be diverted to another purchase. For example, 5,000 points is 50 percent of 10,000 and would be worth $75 toward another purchase. However, do not give your child the reward if he does not earn it. That would eliminate future uses of reinforcement. Likewise, do not deny or postpone the goal once it is earned. The system described above is not in

concrete. It should be adapted to the age and maturity of the adolescent. One youngster would be insulted by an approach that would thrill another.

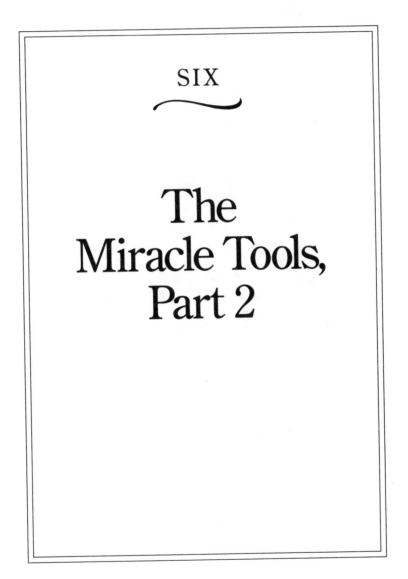

SIX

The Miracle Tools, Part 2

As we have been discussing, increasing a child's level of responsibility and self-discipline is not a simple task. It must be taught by parents with a specific game plan. But the job is made easier by utilizing the Law of Reinforcement. In the previous chapter, we examined two specific principles which maximize the benefits of this technique. These were to (1) grant rewards immediately, and also (2) utilize nonmaterial rewards, such as praise, hugs, and plain old attentiveness, along with financial and material reinforcement.

We'll turn our attention now to the remaining three principles, beginning with this:

3. *Almost any behavior that is learned through reinforcement can be eliminated if the reward is withheld long enough.*

It is an established fact that unreinforced behavior will eventually disappear. This process, called *extinction* by psychologists, can be very useful to parents and teachers who want to alter the behavior of children.

Again, the animal world provides many interesting examples of extinction. For example, the walleyed pike is a large fish with a big appetite for minnows. If placed in a tank of water with its small prey, the pike will soon be in the tank alone. However, an interesting thing occurs when a plate of glass is slipped into the tank, separating the pike from the minnows. The pike cannot see the glass and hits it solidly in pursuit of its dinner. Again and again it will swim into the glass, bumping whatever one calls the front end of a walleyed pike. Clearly, behavior is *not* being reinforced, and, thus, is extinguished gradually.

Eventually, the pike gives up. It has learned that the minnows are not available. The glass can then be taken from the tank, allowing the minnows to swim around their mortal enemy in perfect safety. The pike will not try to eat them. It knows what it knows: They are unreachable. Amazingly, the walleyed pike will actually starve to death while its favorite food casually swims right past its mouth.

Extinction is also utilized to restrain elephants in a circus. When the elephant is young, its foot is chained to a large, immovable cement block. The animal will pull repeatedly against the barrier without success, thereby extinguishing its escape behavior. Later, a small rope attached to a fragile stake from which a dog could break free will be sufficient to restrain the powerful pachyderm. Again, the beast knows what it knows!

Let me say it once more: Children are human and unlike the animal world in most respects. But the principle of extinction is applicable to kids, as well. To eliminate an undesirable behavior in a child, one must identify and then withhold the critical reinforcement. Let's apply this concept to a common childhood problem. Why does a child whine instead of speaking in a normal voice? Because the parent has reinforced whining! When three-year-old Karen speaks in her usual voice, her mom is too busy to listen. Actually, Karen babbles all day long, so her mother tunes out most of her verbiage. But when Karen speaks in a grating, irritating, obnoxious tone, Mom turns to see what's wrong. Karen's whining brings results; her normal voice does not. And so she becomes a whiner.

To extinguish the whining, one must simply reverse the reinforcement. Mom should begin by saying, "I can't hear you because you're whining, Karen. I have funny ears. They just can't hear whining." After this message has been communicated for a day or two, Mom should ignore all moan-tones. On the other hand, she should offer immediate attention to a request made in a normal voice.

If this control of reinforcement is applied properly, it *will* achieve the desired results. Nearly all learning is based on this principle, and the consequences are certain and predictable. Of course, Grandma and Uncle Albert may continue to reinforce the behavior you are trying to extinguish, and thereby keep it alive. So teamwork is a must, especially between parents.

Extinction is not only a tool for use in a deliberate training program. It also happens accidentally at times. Consider the case of four-year-old Mark. His mother and father were concerned about his temper tantrums, especially since he habitually threw them when his parents least wanted him to misbehave. For example, when guests were visiting in their home, he would explode just before bedtime. The same outbursts occurred in restaurants, church services, and other public places.

Mark's parents were no strangers to discipline, and they tried every approach on their little rebel. They spanked him, stood him in the corner, sent him to bed early, and shamed and scolded him. Nothing worked. The temper tantrums continued regularly.

Then one evening Mark's parents were both reading a newspaper in their living room. They had said something that angered their son, and he fell on the floor in a rage. He screamed and whacked his head on the carpet, kicking and flailing his small arms. They were totally exasperated at that point and didn't know what to do, so they did nothing. They continued reading the paper in stony silence, which was the last thing the little tornado expected. He got up, looked at his father, and fell down for Act Two. Again his parents made no response. By this time they were glancing at one another knowingly and watching junior with curiosity. Again, Mark's tantrum stopped abruptly. He approached his mother, shook her arm, then collapsed for Act Three. They continued ignoring him. His response? This child felt so silly flapping and crying on the floor that he never threw another tantrum.

Now it can be told: The illustration cited above was included in the first edition of *Dare to Discipline*, back in 1970. It is time now to reveal that Mark was not the real name of that child. It was Jim. Alas, *I* was the brat in the story. And I can tell you, it's no fun staging a performance if the crowd won't come!

It is clear that the reinforcement for my tantrums was parental manipulation. Through violent behavior, I had gotten those big, powerful adults upset and distraught. I must have loved it. With most children, tantrums are a form of challenging behavior that can be eliminated by one or more appropriate spankings. For a few like me, however, something else was going on. Like a pyromaniac, I enjoyed seeing how much commotion I could precipitate. That, in itself, was my reward.

Although my parents extinguished this negative behavior in one episode, it usually takes much longer. It is important to understand the typical rate at which a characteristic will disappear without reinforcement.

Consider again the example of the pigeon checking radio parts, mentioned in the previous chapter. Initially, the bird missed all the defective components, and only gradually recognized a higher percentage. As illustrated in Figure A, the pigeon eventually identified 100 percent of the parts, and continued with perfect accuracy while the reinforcement (grain) was paid for each success.

Suppose the reinforcement was then withheld. The pigeon would continue to intercept the broken parts with perfect accuracy, but not for long. Soon he would begin to miss a few bad components. If he continued to work for nothing, he would become more and more distracted and disinterested in his task. By the end of the day, he would miss all or most of the defective parts.

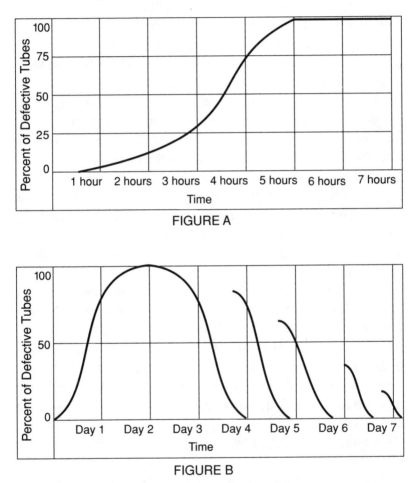

FIGURE A

FIGURE B

However, the following day, he would again go to work as before. *Even though the behavior is extinguished one day, it will likely return the next.* This reawakening is called "spontaneous recovery." Each day, the behavior returns as illustrated in

Figure B. But the accuracy is less and the daily extinction occurs more quickly than the day before.

This principle is important in extinguishing undesirable behavior in children. A parent or teacher should not become discouraged if an extinguished behavior reappears. Its complete elimination may require considerable time.

The principle of extinction has helped many people break bad habits. One such system is designed for those who want to quit smoking. It is based on eliminating the pleasantness (reinforcement) usually produced by inhaling cigarette smoke. To do this, a tube filled with very stale, concentrated tobacco smoke is aimed at the smoker's face. Whenever the individual takes a puff from his cigarette, he is shot in the face with the putrid smoke from the tube. The smoker begins to associate cigarettes with the foul blast in his face, and by this means sometimes develops a strong dislike for smoking. Unfortunately, nicotine is one of the most addictive narcotics known, and the chemical impact is extremely difficult to overcome.

Extinction can also help children overcome some of their unnecessary fears. I once consulted with a mother who was very concerned about her three-year-old daughter's fear of the dark. Despite the use of a night light and leaving the bedroom door open, little Marla was afraid to stay in her room alone. She insisted that her mother sit with her until she went to sleep each evening, which was extremely time-consuming and inconvenient. If Marla happened to awaken in the night, she would call for help. It was apparent that she was genuinely frightened.

Fears such as these are not innate: they have been learned. If parents truly realized this, they would be more careful about what they say and how they act. The fact is, youngsters are amazingly perceptive and often adopt the behaviors and concerns they see in adults. Even good-natured teasing can produce problems for a child. If a youngster walks into a dark room and is pounced upon from behind the door, he quickly learns that the dark is not always empty!

In Marla's case, it was unclear where she learned to fear the dark, but I believe her mother inadvertently magnified the problem. In her concern for her daughter, she conveyed anxiety, and Marla began to think her own fears must be justified. "Even mother is worried about it," she undoubtedly reasoned. Marla became so frightened that she could not walk through a dimly lit room without an escort. It was at this point that she was referred to me.

Since it is usually unfruitful to try to talk children out of their fears, I suggested that the mother *show* Marla there was nothing to be afraid of. That would help the child perceive her mother as being confident and unthreatened. So she bought a bag of candy (okay, okay . . . I would use pieces of the popular rolled-up fruit today) and placed her chair just outside Marla's bedroom door. Marla was then offered a piece of candy if she spent a few seconds in her bedroom with the light on and door shut. This first step was not very threatening, and Marla enjoyed the game. It was repeated several times, and then she was asked to walk several feet into the darkened room while her mother, clearly visible in the hall, counted to ten. This was also easy, and Marla continued playing along for the bits of candy.

On subsequent trips, the door was shut a few inches more and the lights were lowered. Finally, Marla had the courage to enter the dark room and shut the door while her mother counted to three—then five—then eight. The time in the dark was gradually lengthened, and instead of producing fear it produced candy: ultimate pleasure to a small child. She also heard her mother talking confidently and quietly, and knew she could come out whenever she wished. Through these means, courage was reinforced and fear extinguished.

Like the kind of reward you choose, the uses of extinction are limited only by the imagination and creativity of the parent or teacher. Try it in various settings. With a little practice and patience, you will see for yourself that one of the best methods of changing a behavior is to withhold reinforcement while rewarding its replacement.

Moving ahead, the fourth principle of getting the most from the miracle tool is:

4. *Parents and teachers are also vulnerable to reinforcement.* Reinforcement is not only the mechanism by which *children* and *animals* learn new behavior. Adults also modify their behavior according to the positive and negative feedback they receive. Inevitably children sometimes train their parents, rather than the reverse, by reinforcing certain behaviors and extinguishing others.

For example, when Mom and Dad take their children to some exciting place, such as Disneyland, the youngsters put on their best behavior. They may be sweet and cooperative— an unsubtle attempt to reinforce or reward their parents' action. In extreme cases, I have seen children adeptly manipulate their parents to get what they want or the behavior they prefer.

A case in point is when Mom disciplines her eight-year-old daughter, only to hear, "You don't love me anymore." Most children know their parents are anxious to convey their love, so they use this delicate issue to extinguish punishment. It often succeeds.

Another example is when the teacher announces, "It is time to study health, so get out your textbooks," and the entire class groans. For some instructors, this lack of reinforcement is difficult to tolerate, and they'll either eliminate a boring subject from their future curriculum or teach it in the most perfunctory way.

Similar phenomena occur in higher education, too. I knew of a graduate school psychology class in which the students experimented with reinforcement on their professor. This instructor utilized two distinct teaching methods. He either lectured from his notes, which was a dry, dismal experience for students, or he spoke extemporaneously, resulting in lively and interesting discussions. One day the students agreed before class to reward his conversational style and extinguish his formal behavior. Whenever he used notes, they shuffled their feet, looked out the window, yawned and whispered to each other. On the other hand, they exhibited fascination with his unstructured lessons. The professor responded in classic fashion. He adopted the informal approach almost exclusively, although he didn't know he was being manipulated until nearly the end of the semester.

A final example is the dad who has a very low frustration tolerance with his children. He screams at them whenever they fall short of his expectations, which seems to make them obey. He has been reinforced for his screaming and becomes a loud, aggressive parent.

The point is simple: Parents should be aware of their own reactions to reinforcement and make certain they are in control of the learning situation.

The fifth and final key of the Law of Reinforcement is:

5. *Parents often reinforce undesirable behavior and weaken behavior they value.*

Perhaps the most important aspect of the past two chapters relates to accidental reinforcement. It is remarkably easy to reward undesirable behavior in children by allowing it to succeed. Suppose, for example, that Mr. and Mrs. Weakknee are having dinner guests, and they put three-year-old Ricky to bed at seven o'clock. They know Ricky will cry, as he always does, but what else can they do? Indeed, Ricky cries. He begins at a low pitch and gradually builds to the decibel level of a jet at takeoff.

Finally, Mrs. Weakknee becomes so embarrassed by the display that she lets Ricky get up. What has the child learned? That he must cry *loudly* if he doesn't want to go to bed. Quiet protests don't work. Mr. and Mrs. Weakknee had better be prepared for a tearful battle the following night, too, because the response eventually succeeded. And if they forget, Ricky will undoubtedly remind them.

To explain this principle further, let's consider another scenario. An argumentative teenager, Laura Beth, never takes "no" for an answer. She is so cantankerous that she's only homesick when she's home. Whenever her mother is unsure whether she should allow Laura Beth to go out at night, she first tells her she *can't* go. By saying "no" initially, Laura Beth's mom buys some extra time to think the request over. She can always change her mind, but she knows it's easier to go from "no" to "yes" than the other way. However, what all of this tells Laura Beth is that "no" really means "maybe" . . . and that "yes" is possible if she argues and complains enough.

Many parents make the same mistake as Laura Beth's mother. They allow arguing, sulking, pouting, door slamming and bargaining to succeed. Parents should not take a definitive position on an issue until they have thought it over thoroughly and listened to the child's argument. Then they should stick tenaciously to their decision. If the teenager learns that "no" means "absolutely not," she is less likely to waste her effort appealing her case.

Or suppose it is Mr. and Mrs. Smith's tenth wedding anniversary and they are going out for dinner. As they prepare to leave, their five- and six-year-old children begin howling about being left behind. Mr. Smith is vaguely familiar with the principles of reinforcement, so he offers a pack of gum to the children if they'll stop crying. Unfortunately, Mr. Smith has not reinforced the silence; he has rewarded the tears. The next time he and Mrs. Smith leave it will be to the children's advantage to cry again. A small alternative would have changed the setting entirely. Mr. Smith should have offered the gum for their cooperation before the tears began to fall.

Let's apply the principle to babies and their tears. Crying is an important form of communication for infants. Through their wails we learn of their hunger, fatigue, discomfort, or diaper disaster. Although we don't want to eliminate crying in babies, it is possible to make them less fussy by minimizing the reinforcement of their tears. If an infant is immediately picked up or rocked each time he cries, he may quickly observe the relationship between tears and adults' attention. How well I remember standing at the doorway of my infant daughter's nursery for several minutes, awaiting a momentary lull in the crying before going to her crib. By doing so, I reinforced the pauses rather than the howls.

Obviously, parents must be careful about the behaviors they allow to succeed. They must exercise self-discipline and patience to ensure that the tools of reinforcement and extinction are being used to encourage responsible and mature behavior.

QUESTIONS AND ANSWERS

Q *How can I acquaint my junior higher with the need for responsible behavior throughout his life? He is desperately in need of this understanding.*

A Rather than reinvent the wheel, let me again quote from one of my other books which addresses this very issue. There, I said the overall objective during preadolescence is teaching the child that actions have inevitable consequences. One of the most serious casualties in a permissive society is the failure to connect those two factors: behavior and consequences.

Too often, a three-year-old child screams insults at his mother, but Mom stands blinking her eyes in confusion. A first grader launches an attack on his teacher, but the school makes allowances for his age and takes no action. A ten-year-old is caught stealing CDs in a store, but is released to the recognizance of his parents. A fifteen-year-old sneaks the keys to the family car, but his father pays the fine when he is arrested. A seventeen-year-old drives his Chevy like a maniac and his parents pay for the repairs when he tears off the front fender. You see, all through childhood, loving parents seem determined to intervene between behavior and consequences, breaking the connection and preventing the valuable learning that could have occurred.

Thus, it is possible for a young man or woman to enter adulthood without knowing that life bites—that every move we make directly affects our future, and that irresponsible behavior eventually produces sorrow and pain. Such a person applies for his first job and arrives late for work three times during the first week. Later, when fired in a flurry of hot words, he becomes bitter and frustrated. It was the first time in his life that Mom and Dad couldn't come running to rescue him from the unpleasant consequences. Unfortunately, many North American parents still "bail out" their children long after they are grown and living away from home. What is the result? This overprotection produces emotional cripples who often develop lasting characteristics of dependency and a kind of perpetual adolescence.

How does one connect behavior with consequences? By being willing to let the child experience a reasonable amount of pain or inconvenience when he behaves irresponsibly.

When Barbara misses the school bus through her own daw-dling, let her walk a mile or two and enter school in midmorn-ing (unless safety factors prevent this). If Janie carelessly loses her lunch money, let her skip a meal. Obviously, it is possible to carry this principle too far and become harsh and inflexible with an immature child. The best approach is to expect boys and girls to carry the responsibility that is appro-priate for their age and occasionally to taste the bitter fruit that irresponsibility bears.

Q *You have referred to children who manipulate their mothers and fathers. On the other hand, isn't the parent manip-ulating the child by the use of rewards and punishment?*

A No more than a factory supervisor is manipulating his employees by insisting that they arrive at work by 9:00 A.M. No more than a policeman manipulates the speeding driver by giving him a traffic ticket. No more than an insurance company manipulates that same driver by increasing his premium. No more than the IRS manipulates a taxpayer who files his return one day late and pays a penalty for his tardiness. The word "manipulation" implies a sinister or selfish motive. I prefer the term "leadership," which is in the best interest of everyone—even when it involves unpleasant consequences.[1]

Q *I am a teacher in junior high school, and there are five separate classes that come to my room to be taught science each day. My biggest problem is getting those students to bring books, paper, and pencils to class with them. I can lend them the equipment they need, but I never get it back. What do you suggest?*

A I faced an identical problem the year I taught junior high school. My students were not malicious; they just had too many other things on their minds to remember to bring their school materials. I tried various motivational techniques, but without success. I appealed to the students' desire for responsibility, but generated only yawns. I launched an emotional tirade, but that seemed like a great waste of energy for such a small issue. There had to be a better way!

I finally reached a solution based on the certainty that young people will cooperate if it's to their advantage. I announced one morning that I no longer cared whether they brought their pencils and books to class. I had twenty extra books and several boxes of sharpened pencils which they could borrow. If they forgot to bring these materials, all they had to do was ask for a loan. I would not gnash my teeth or get red in the face; they would find me very willing to share my resources.

However, there was one catch. The borrowing student had to stand beside his desk (or lean over if written work was require) for that one-hour period. I smiled to myself in subsequent days as the kids raced around before class, trying to scrounge up books or pencils from friends. Two hundred and twenty students came to my classroom every day, and yet I only had to enforce the "standing" rule about once a week. The pupils watched out for their own best interests. One lapse in their memory was all it took; they didn't blunder into the same situation twice.

At the risk of being redundant, I will repeat the valuable formula for managing children and teenagers: give them maximum reason to comply with your wishes. Your anger is the *least* effective motivation I can imagine.

Q *If rewards and punishment should be given very quickly, why does God not interact that way with us, His children? People seem to "get away" with bad behavior for years, and the ultimate reward for those who live a Christian life will come only after death. Surely the Lord knows about "immediate reinforcement."*

A He certainly does. He created the characteristics we only observe and try to understand. So why does He not reinforce the behavior He desires more quickly? I don't know, although that fact is acknowledged in Scripture: "When the sentence for a crime is not quickly carried out, the hearts of the people are filled with schemes to do wrong. Although a wicked man commits a hundred crimes and still lives a long time, I know that it will go better with God-fearing men, who are reverent before God" (Ecclesiastes 8:11-12, NIV).

Whether they arrive on time or not, the warnings and promises in Scripture are more reliable than anything else in the universe. He *will* have the last word!

Q *What is your opinion of the juvenile courts? Do they reward good behavior and extinguish bad? Are they efficient in discouraging delinquency?*

A Not generally, but the blame is difficult to locate. I served for three years on President Ronald Reagan's National Advisory Commission to the Office of Juvenile Justice and Delinquency Prevention. It was a fascinating, although occasionally discouraging assignment. I observed that the courts build delinquents in some cases as systematically as if they were placing stone on stone.

This happened with a ninth grader I knew who had broken every rule he could violate, just to demonstrate the toothlessness of the law. Craig would brag to his friends before committing an illegal act, and then laugh when he was not punished. In a matter of two years' time, he had stolen two cars and one motorcycle, had run away from home twice, was suspended from school three times, and was arrested once as a peeping Tom. I watched him march off to court repeatedly where he was released after receiving another worn-out lecture from the judge.

Finally, Craig was sent to a camp for delinquent boys where he wrote me a letter saying how he regretted the mess he'd made of his life. He was anxious to get home and take advantage of his educational opportunity. I think Craig wanted to know how far he could push "John Law." As soon as he got the answer, he no longer wanted to fight. He should have been punished the first time he was arrested.

Shortly after hearing from Craig, I talked to a well-known judge about the obvious leniency of the courts. I asked him why juvenile authorities are so reluctant to take action against a defiant teenager, even though he may be begging for punishment. The judge cited two reasons for the attitudes of his colleagues:

(1) There aren't enough correctional facilities available for boys like Craig. The work camps must be reserved for the greatest troublemakers.

(2) It is difficult for judges to get excited about milder forms of delinquency when they have been dealing with more serious cases involving murder, rape, and robbery. It is unfortunate that the judges are limited in this fashion. A teenager's first encounter with the law should be so painful that he would not want to make the same mistake again, but our legal apparatus is not designed to accomplish that objective.

The juvenile courts occasionally commit the opposite error of dealing too harshly with a teenager. Such had been the case with Linda, a girl I met late one rainy afternoon. I was working on a report at my desk when I suddenly realized I was not alone. I looked up to see a barefoot, rain-soaked girl in my doorway. She was a pretty adolescent of about fifteen years.

"You can call the police now," she instructed me.

"Why would I want to call the police?" I asked.

"Because I have run away from ———." (She named a nearby detention home for delinquent girls.) She said she'd spent the day hiding from the authorities.

She told me her name was Linda, and I asked her to sit down and tell me why she had run away. She started at the beginning, and I later verified the facts to be true. Her mother had been a prostitute who gave no supervision or guidance to her daughter. Linda was even allowed to remain in the bedroom while her mother entertained men. The child was eventually taken away from her mother and made a ward of the court. She was placed in a home for young victims where there was not enough love to go around. Her mother came to see her for a few years, but then ignored her completely.

Linda was so starved for love that she ran away to find her mother. She was immediately returned to the home. A year later she tried to escape again, with the same result. Linda continued to run away, each time becoming more sophisticated in evading the police. The year before my introduction to this girl, she had vanished again, this time being picked up by several boys. They lived together for two weeks and were involved in several misdemeanors and various sexual escapades during that period.

Linda was subsequently arrested and brought before the juvenile court as a delinquent. She was sentenced to the detention center for delinquent girls, surrounded by ten-foot chain link fences. The court considered her to be an unmanageable, incorrigible adolescent, yet this was wrong. Linda was a lonely, love-starved girl who had been cheated by the circumstances of life. She needed someone to care—not someone to punish. Perhaps the judge was too busy to study her background; perhaps he had no alternative facility for Linda. Either way, the needs of this wispy girl remained unmet at this critical time of her life.

Juvenile justice must be designed to be lenient with the child who has been hurt, like Linda, and to sting the child who has challenged authority, like Craig. It is sometimes difficult to recognize the difference.

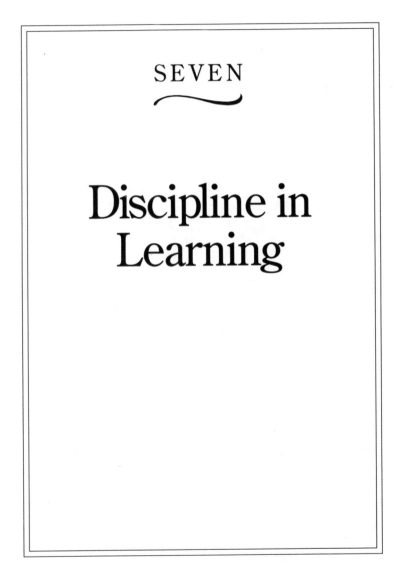

SEVEN

Discipline in Learning

W hen I was in college, there was a malicious little rumor going around that an amazing discovery had been made about human learning. A new technique called "sleep teaching" made it possible to cram one's head full of facts while sawing the logs. I have to tell you that idea was very appealing to me. It would have fit into my program perfectly to do the big-man-on-campus thing during the day and accomplish my studying while dreaming. Also being a psychology major, I was interested in brain function and promptly set out to test the hypothesis.

I selected a class in which three tests were given during the semester with the lowest score being dropped by the professor. I studied hard on the first two exams and earned respectable grades, which permitted me to experiment with the third. When the exam was scheduled, I recorded all the necessary factual information on my tape machine, being careful not to learn the detail as I spoke into the microphone. In all, about sixty minutes of data were packed on one side of an old reel to reel tape. Then I went out and enjoyed myself the night before the test. While my brighter friends were grinding away in the library, I was shooting the breeze in a restaurant with some guys who never studied much anyway. It felt wonderful.

At bedtime that night, I plugged the tape recorder into my clock radio so that my own voice would begin speaking to my unconscious mind at two o'clock in the morning. One hour later, I was awakened by the flopping of the tape at the end of the reel, and I reset the timer for four o'clock. The tape played for another hour and awakened me again at five. The final "hearing" occurred between six and seven. So passed the restless night.

The examination was scheduled for eight o'clock and I was there, yawning and bleary-eyed. The first thing I noted was that the questions on the printed test were not even vaguely familiar to me (always a bad sign). But I was still confident that the information was stored down deep in my brain, somewhere. I turned in the test and stood waiting for a proctor to calculate my score. It only took a few minutes.

There were seventy-three people in the class, and I got the seventy-second-lowest score. I managed to beat the class dummy by one point, but he appealed to the professor over a disputed answer and was granted two additional points. I came in dead last! The only thing I got from that experiment was a terrible night's sleep and the wrath of a roommate who had lain there in the moonlight learning junk he didn't want to know.

Many years have passed since those days of my callow youth when I still thought getting something for nothing was possible. I was dead wrong. Everything worth having comes with a price. The natural progression of the universe is movement from order to chaos, not the other way around. The only way to beat that curse is to invest energy into a project or objective. If improvement is to be made in anything, *especially* in the development of mental skills and knowledge, it will be accomplished through blood, sweat, and a few tears. There's no way around it.

It is my belief that some, but by no means all, professional educators began to lose sight of that need for discipline in learning as we came through the turbulent sixties. They enthusiastically searched for an easier way to teach kids than putting them through the rigors of structured classrooms, examinations, grades, rules, and requirements. Society was changing, authority went out of style, and all the traditional values began to look suspect. Why not throw out convention and try something new? How about—an "open" classroom?

One of the most foolish ideas in the history of education was born. Let me cite excerpts from an article appearing in the *Seattle News Journal,* May 27, 1971, describing an open classroom in its full glory. Before doing so, however, let me emphasize that the excesses of the past are no longer evident in today's public schools. I'm hearing good things about the Seattle School District, for example, that experimented back in 1971 with the unstructured program described below. If those days have past, then why do we focus on a time when schools went off the deep end? Because we can't fully understand who we are today without examining where we've been. And because we can learn from the excesses of yesterday, when authority and discipline were distrusted. And because the remnants of this free-wheeling philosophy still lurk within our permissive society and the halls of academia.

The article referred to above was called "The School Nobody Talks About", and was written by James and John Flaherty. As you read the following excerpts, imagine your own child enrolled in a program of this nature.

❖　　❖　　❖

Picture if you can, five- to twelve-year-olds riding tricycles down the school hall, painting on the walls, as they wish and what they wish, doing what they want to and when they want, communicating openly with their teachers in three- and four-letter words, dictating school policy, teaching, and curriculum as they wish. And all of this in a public school in Seattle! Far out or impossible? No! Its happening right now in conservative old Seward Park. And the Seattle School District is picking up the tab.

The Elementary Alternative School is an experimental project of the school district. It began in November 1970 and was founded on the premise that regular elementary schools are too restrictive. It was cited that a school should teach the child to learn in a more natural environment and that his motivations to learn should arise from within himself. Also, that a child of any age is capable of making his own decisions and should be allowed to do so.

It's a kid's paradise. There is no formal curriculum, no age barriers, no classroom structure, no overall program. In fact, if the child doesn't want to learn the three Rs he doesn't have to.

On our tour, no formal classwork was being conducted. The children seemed to mill aimlessly in the three unkept classrooms. Apparently no class was in session. Then we entered the basement of the building next door . . . to consult with Mr. Bernstein (who directs the school). Bernstein . . . pointed out that this was a "fully new concept in learning, as exemplified by A. S. Neill at Springhill, a progressive school in eastern U.S." Bernstein said that four-letter words are often used to get attention or hammer home a point in his college classes, and he didn't see that it would harm any of the children in the Alternative School. "You have to communicate with children in the language they understand," he said.

Bernstein [was] queried on the fact that no formal classes were kept, no grades given, and therefore, how could a pupil finishing the sixth grade enter a regular school. "In six years," Bernstein replied, "perhaps all our schools will be like this one, and there'll be no problem."

Not many school districts experimented with programs as extreme as this one, fortunately, but the tenor of the times held authority and discipline in contempt. A depressing example of that changing philosophy was spelled out in a widely published book entitled *Summerhill,* by A. S. Neill, to whom Mr. Bernstein referred. I was required to read this ridiculous book while in graduate school. It contradicted everything I believed about children, and indeed, about life itself. But Neill's writings and work were given great credibility in educational circles, and many teachers and principals (like Bernstein) were influenced by his laissez-faire philosophy.

Summerhill in England and Springhill in the U.S. were permissive institutions that conformed to the easy-come, easy-go philosophy of their superintendent, A. S. Neill. Resident students were not required to get out of bed in the morning, attend classes, complete assignments, take baths, or even wear clothes. Rarely in human history have children been given wider latitude.

Let me list the elements of Neill's philosophy that governed his much-vaunted program and which he recommended with great passion to parents the world over:

1. Adults have no right to insist on obedience from their children. Attempts to make the youngsters obey are merely designed to satisfy the adult's desire for power. There is no excuse for imposing parental wishes on children. They must be free. The best home situation is one where parents and children are perfect equals. A child should be required to do nothing until he *chooses* to do so. Neill went to great lengths to show the students that he was one of them—not their superior.

2. Children must not be asked to work at all until they reach eighteen years of age. Parents should not even require them to help with small errands or assist with the chores. We insult them by making them do our menial tasks. Neill actually stressed the importance of withholding responsibility from the child.

3. Religion should not be taught to children. The only reason religion exists in society is to release the false guilt it has generated over sexual matters. Our concepts of God, heaven, hell, and sin are based on myths. Enlightened generations of the future will reject traditional religion.

4. Punishment of any kind is strictly forbidden, according to Neill's philosophy. A parent who spanks his child

actually hates him, and his desire to hurt the child results from his own unsatisfied sex life. At Summerhill, one young student broke seventeen windows without receiving so much as a verbal reprimand.

5. Adolescents should be told sexual promiscuity is not a moral issue at all. At Summerhill, premarital intercourse was not sanctioned only because Neill feared the consequences of public indignation. He and members of his staff sometimes went nude to eliminate sexual curiosity. He predicted that the adolescents of tomorrow would find a more healthy existence through an unrestricted sex life. (What they found was a disease called AIDS and a firsthand knowledge of other sexually transmitted diseases.)

6. No pornographic books or materials should be withheld from the child. Neill indicated that he would buy filthy literature for any of his students who wished to have it. This, he felt, would cure their prurient interests—without harming the child.

7. Children should not be required to say "thank you" or "please" to their parents. Further, they should not even be encouraged to do so.

8. Rewarding a child for good behavior is a degrading and demoralizing practice. It is an unfair form of coercion.

9. Neill considered books to be insignificant in a school. Education should consist largely of work with clay, paint, tools, and various forms of drama. Learning is not without value, but it should come after play.

10. Even if a child fails in school, the matter should never be mentioned by his parents. The child's activities are strictly his business.

11. Neill's philosophy, in brief, was as follows: Eliminate all authority; let the child grow without outside interference; don't instruct him; don't force anything on him.

If A. S. Neill had been the only lonely proponent of this assault on authority, he would not have been worthy of concern. To the contrary, he represented an extreme example of a view that became very widely accepted in educational circles. Herbert R. Kohn authored *The Open Classroom* and helped give respectability to a somewhat more sane version of the concept in public schools. Believe it or not, this was "cutting edge" stuff for more than a decade. We've now had twenty-five years to evaluate the fallout from the lessening of discipline and authority in the classroom. Look at what happened to the generation that was influenced most by it.

They concluded in the late sixties that God was dead, that immorality was the new morality, that disrespect and irreverence were proper, that unpopular laws were to be disobeyed, that violence was an acceptable vehicle for bringing change, (as were their childhood tantrums), that authority was evil, that pleasure was paramount, that older people were not to be trusted, that diligence was distasteful, and that their country was unworthy of allegiance or respect. Every one of those components can be linked to the philosophy taught by A. S. Neill, but also believed by many of his contemporaries. It cost us a generation of our best and brightest, many of whom still suffer from the folly of their youth!

Not only did the misguided philosophy set up the student revolution of the late sixties. It also caused serious damage to our school system and the kids who became the victims of it. I was a young teacher at the time and was shocked to see the lack of order and control in some of my colleagues' classrooms. The confusion was evident at every grade level. Tiny first graders cowed their harassed teachers as systematically as did the boisterous high school students. In some situations, entire classes became so proficient at disrupting order that they were dreaded and feared by their future teachers. It seemed ridiculous for school officials to tolerate such disobedience when it could have been easily avoided. However, in instances when the educators did exercise firmness, many parents protested and demanded leniency for their children.

I have lived long enough, now, to have followed some of those kids into adult life. I've talked to them personally. I've read their testimonials. I've felt their anger. One of the most poignant statements I've seen was written in the "My Turn" section of *Newsweek* magazine, August 30, 1976. The author, Mara Wolynski, was a product of the philosophy I have been describing. Her story, "Confessions of a Misspent Youth," tells it all.

❖   ❖   ❖

The idea of permissive education appealed to my mother in 1956 when she was a Bohemian and I was four. In Greenwich Village, she found a small private school whose beliefs were hers and happily enrolled me. I know it was an act of motherly love but it might have been the worst thing she ever did to me. This school — I'll call it Sand and Sea—attracted other such parents, upper-middle-class professionals who were determined not to have their children pressured the way they had been. Sand and Sea was the school without pain. And it was the kind of school that the back-to-basics people rightly fear most. At Sand and Sea, I soon became an exemplar of educational freedom—the freedom not to learn.

Sand and Sea was run by fifteen women and one man who taught "science." They were decent people, some old, some young, and all devoted to cultivating the innate creativity they were convinced we had. There was a tremendous emphasis on the arts. We weren't taught techniques, however, because any kind of organization stunted creativity.

Happiness and Hieroglyphics. We had certain hours allotted to various subjects but we were free to dismiss anything that bored us. In fact, it was school policy that we were forbidden to be bored or miserable or made to compete with one another. There were no tests and no hard times. When I was bored with math, I was excused and allowed to write short stories in the library. The way we learned history was by trying to re-create its least important elements. One year, we pounded corn, made tepees, ate buffalo meat, and learned two Indian words. That was early American history. Another year we made elaborate costumes, clay pots, and papier-mâché gods. That was Greek culture. Another year we were all maidens and knights in armor because it was time to learn about the Middle Ages. We drank our orange juice from tin-foil goblets but never found out what the Middle Ages were. They were just 'The Middle Ages.'

I knew that the Huns pegged their horses and drank a quart of blood before going to war, but no one ever told us who the Huns were or why we should know who they were. And one year, the year of ancient Egypt, when we were building our pyramids, I did a thirty-foot-long mural for which I laboriously copied hieroglyphics onto the sheet of brown paper. But no one ever told me what they stood for. They were just there and beautiful.

Ignorance Is Not Bliss. We spent great amounts of time being creative because we had been told by our incurably optimistic mentors that the way to be happy in life was to create. Thus, we didn't learn to read until we were in the third grade, because early reading was thought to discourage creative spontaneity. The one thing they taught us very well was to hate intellectuality and anything connected with it. Accordingly, we were forced to be creative for nine years. And yet Sand and Sea has failed to turn out a good artist. What we did do was to continually form and re-form interpersonal relationships, and that's what we thought learning was all about, and we were happy. At ten, for example, most of us were functionally illiterate, but we could tell that Raymond was "acting out" when, in the middle of what passed for English, he did the twist on top of his desk. Or that Nina was "introverted" because she always cowered in the corner.

When we finally were graduated, however, all the happy little children fell down the hill. We felt a profound sense of abandonment. So did our parents. After all that tuition money, let alone the loving freedom, their children faced high school with all the glorious prospects of the poorest slum-school kids. And so it came to be. No matter what school we went to, we were the underachievers and the culturally disadvantaged.

For some of us, real life was too much—one of my oldest friends from Sand and Sea killed himself two years ago after flunking out of the worst high school in New York at twenty. Various others have put in time in mental institutions where they were free, once again, to create during occupational therapy.

During my own high-school years, the school psychologist was baffled by my lack of substantive knowledge. He suggested to my mother that I be given a battery of psychological tests to find out why I was blocking out information. The thing was, I wasn't blocking because I had no information to block. Most of my Sand and Sea classmates were also enduring the same kinds of hardships that accompany severe handicaps. My own reading comprehension was in the lowest eighth percentile, not surprisingly. I was often asked by teachers how I had gotten into high school. However, I did manage to stumble *not* only through high school but also through college (first junior college—rejected by all four-year colleges, and then New York University), hating it all the way as I had been taught to. I am still amazed that I have a B.A., but think of it as a B.S.

The Lure of Learning. The parents of my former classmates can't figure out what went wrong. They had sent in bright, curious children and gotten back, nine years later, helpless adolescents. Some might say that those of us who freaked out would have freaked out anywhere, but when you see the same bizarre behavior pattern in succeeding graduating classes, you can draw certain terrifying conclusions.

Now I see my twelve-year-old brother (who is in a traditional school) doing college-level math and I know that he knows more about many other things besides math than I do. And I also see traditional education working in the case of my fifteen-year-old brother (who was summarily yanked from Sand and Sea, by my reformed mother, when he was eight so that he wouldn't become like me). Now, after seven years of real education, he is making impressive film documentaries for a project on the Bicentennial. A better learning experience than playing Pilgrim for four and a half

months, and Indian for four and a half months, which is how I
imagine they spent this year at Sand and Sea.

And now I've come to see that the real job of school is to entice
the student into the web of knowledge and then, if he's not enticed, to drag him in. I wish I had been.

It was noble of the *Newsweek* publishers to print this emotional "confession" by Myra Wolynski. After all, the popular
press has been a significant part of the problem, extolling the
virtues of avant-garde trends in the classroom. *Newsweek*
magazine, for example, devoted its May 3, 1971, cover story
to the topic, "Learning Can Be Fun." On the cover was an
elementary school girl making something with papier-mâché.
Four years later, *Newsweek*'s cover story considered "Why
Johnny Can't Write." I wrote the senior editor of *Newsweek*
after the second article appeared, December 8, 1975, and
suggested that maybe there was a link between the two
stories. Perhaps Johnny couldn't write because he spent too
much time having fun in the classroom. I received no reply.

Please understand, I am a supporter of the arts in the
curriculum, and I certainly want the educational process to be
as exciting and as much fun as possible. But children will not
learn reading, writing, and math by doing papier-mâché. And
many of them will not pay the price to learn anything unless
they are required to do so! Some educators have disagreed
with this understanding and postulated that kids will sweat
and study because they have an inner thirst for knowledge.

A former superintendent of public instruction in the state
of California is quoted as saying, "To say that children have
an innate love of learning is as muddle-headed as to say that
children have an innate love of baseball. Some do. Some don't.
Left to themselves, a large percentage of the small fry will go

fishing, pick a fight, tease the girls, or watch Superman on the boob tube. Even as you and I!"

It is a valid observation. Most of the time students will not invest one more ounce of effort in their studies than is required, and that fact has frustrated teachers for hundreds of years. Our schools, therefore, must have enough structure and discipline to *require* certain behavior from their students. This is advantageous not only for academic reasons, but because one of the purposes of education is to prepare the young for later life.

To survive as an adult in this society, one needs to know how to work, how to get there on time, how to get along with others, how to stay with a task until completed, and, yes, how to submit to authority. In short, it takes a good measure of self-discipline and control to cope with the demands of modern living. Maybe one of the greatest gifts a loving teacher can contribute to an immature child, therefore, is to help him learn to sit when he feels like running, to raise his hand when he feels like talking, to be polite to his neighbor, to stand in line without smacking the kid in front, and to do language arts when he feels like doing football.

Likewise, I would hope to see our schools readopt reasonable dress codes, eliminating suggestive clothing, T-shirts with profanity or those promoting heavy metal bands, etc. Guidelines concerning good grooming and cleanliness should also be enforced.

I know! I know! These notions are so alien to us now that we can hardly imagine such a thing. But the benefits would be apparent immediately. Admittedly, hair styles and matters of momentary fashion are of no particular significance, but adherence to a standard is an important element of discipline. The military has understood that for five thousand years! If one examines the secret behind a championship football team, a magnificent orchestra, or a successful business, the principal ingredient is invariably discipline. Thus, it is a great mistake to require nothing of children—to place no demands on their behavior. We all need to adhere to some reasonable rules.

How inaccurate is the belief that self-control is maximized in an environment which places no obligations on its children. How foolish is the assumption that self-discipline is a product of self-indulgence. How unfortunate has been the systematic undermining of educational rules, engineered by a minority of parents through the legal assistance of the American Civil Liberties Union and the tired old judges to whom they have appealed. Despite the will of the majority, the anti-disciplinarians have had their way. The rules governing student conduct have been cut down, and in their place have come a myriad of restrictions on educators. School prayers are illegal even if addressed to an unidentified God. The Bible can be read only as uninspired literature. Allegiance to the flag of our country cannot be required. Educators find it very difficult to punish or expel a student. Teachers are so conscious of parental militancy that they often withdraw from the defiant challenges of their students. As a result, academic discipline lies at the point of death in some of the nation's schools.

The proposal to put standards and reasonable rules back in those schools which have abandoned them (many *haven't*) may sound horribly oppressive to the ears of some Western educators or parents. But it need not be so. Class work *can* be fun and structured at the same time. Indeed, that *is* what happens in Japanese schools, and Russian schools, and English schools. And that's one reason we get whipped when our kids compete against other nations on tests of academic achievement.

You've heard about international achievement tests, of course. You know that our students do poorly when compared to young people from other countries. American high school seniors recently ranked fourteenth out of fifteen countries on a test of advanced algebra skills.[1] Their science scores were lower than those from students in almost every industrialized nation.[2] According to the U.S. Department of Education, only one in five eighth graders has achieved competence for his or her age level.[3] The United States ranks only 49th among 158 member nations of the U.N. in its literacy levels.[4] And SAT scores have been dropping for years.[5]

Before we leap to blame the educators for everything that has gone wrong, however, we need to take another look at the culture. The teachers and school administrators who guide our children have been among the most maligned and under-appreciated people in our society. They are an easy target for abuse. They are asked to do a terribly difficult job, and yet they are criticized almost daily for circumstances beyond their control. Some of their critics act as though educators are deliberately failing our kids. I strongly disagree. We would still be having serious difficulties in our schools if the profes-sionals did everything right. Why? Because what goes on in the classroom cannot be separated from the problems occur-ring in society at large.

Educators certainly can't be blamed for the condition our kids are in when they arrive at school each day. It's not the teachers' fault that families are unraveling and that large numbers of their students have been sexually and/or physi-cally abused, neglected, and undernourished. They can't keep kids from watching mindless television or R-rated videos until midnight, or from using illegal substances or alcohol. In essence, when the culture begins to crumble from massive social problems that defy solutions, the schools will also look bad. That's why even though I disagree with many of the trends in modern education, I sympathize with the dedicated teachers and principals out there who are trying to do the impossible on behalf of our youngsters. They are discouraged today, and they need our support.

Still, there are steps that could be taken to reverse the errors of the past and create a more conducive climate for learning. At the secondary level, we can and *must* make schools a safer place for students *and* teachers. Guns, drugs, and adolescence make a deadly cocktail. It is unbelievable what we have permitted to happen on our campuses. No wonder some kids can't think about their studies. Their *lives* are in danger! Yes, we can reduce the violence if we're committed to the task. Armed guards? Maybe. Metal detectors? If necessary. More expulsions? Probably. No-nonsense administrators? Definitely. Schools with strong leadership, like Joe Clark at Eastside High School in Paterson, New Jersey, have made dramatic progress in improving the academic environment. Above all, we must do what is required to pacify the combat zones in junior and senior high schools.

We will not solve our pervasive problems, however, with the present generation of secondary school students. Our best hope long-term is to start over with the youngsters just coming into elementary school. We can rewrite the rules with these wide-eyed kids. Let's redesign the primary grades to include a greater measure of discipline. I'm not talking merely about more difficult assignments and additional homework. I'm recommending more structure and control in the classroom.

As the first official voice of the school, the primary teacher is in a position to construct positive attitudinal foundations on which future educators can build, or conversely, she can fill her young pupils with contempt and disrespect. A child's teachers during the first six years will largely determine the nature of his attitude toward authority and the educational climate in junior and senior high school (and beyond).

As indicated earlier, I taught school for several years before completing my graduate training and learned more about how children think from that daily exposure than could ever have been assimilated from a textbook. It was also enlightening to observe the disciplinary techniques utilized by other teachers. Some of them exercised perfect classroom control with little effort, while others faced the perpetual humiliation of student defiance. I observed that there was a fundamental difference in the way they approached their classes.

The unskilled teacher would stand in front of the boys and girls and immediately seek their affection. Although most good teachers want to be liked by their classes, some are very dependent on the acceptance of the children. On the first day of school in September, the new teacher, Miss Peach, gives the class a little talk which conveys this message: "I'm so glad we had a chance to get together. This is going to be such a fun year for you; we're going to make soap, and soup, and we're going to paint a mural that will cover that entire wall. We'll take field trips and play games . . . this is going to be a great year. You're going to love me and I'm going to love you, and we'll just have a ball."

Her curriculum is well saturated with fun, fun, fun activities, which are her tokens of affection to the class. All goes well the first day of school, because the students are a little intimidated by the start of a new academic year. But about three days later, little Butch is sitting over at the left and he wants to know what everyone else is questioning too: How far can we push Miss Peach? He is anxious to make a name for himself as a brave toughie, and he might be able to build his reputation at Miss Peach's expense.

At a well-calculated moment, he challenges her with a small act of defiance. Now the last thing Miss Peach wants is conflict, because she had hoped to avoid that sort of thing this year. She does not accept Butch's challenge; she pretends not to notice that he didn't do what she told him to do. He wins this first minor confrontation. Everyone in the class saw what happened: it wasn't a big deal, but Butch survived unscathed.

The next day, Matthew has been greatly encouraged by Butch's success. Shortly after the morning flag salute, he defies her a little more openly than Butch did, and Miss Peach again ignores the challenge. From that moment forward, chaos begins to grow and intensify. Two weeks later Miss Peach is beginning to notice that things are not going very well. She's doing a lot of screaming each day and doesn't know how it got started; she certainly didn't intend to be an angry teacher. By February, life has become intolerable in her classroom; every new project she initiates is sabotaged by her lack of control. And then the thing she wanted least begins to happen: the students openly reveal their contempt for her. They call her names; they laugh at her weaknesses. If she has a physical flaw, such as a large nose or poor eyesight, they point this out to her regularly. Miss Peach cries quietly at recess time, and her head throbs and pounds late into the night. The principal comes in and witnesses the anarchy, and he says, "Miss Peach, you must get control of this class!" But Miss Peach doesn't know how to get control because she doesn't know how she lost it.

It has been estimated that 80 percent of the teachers who quit their jobs after the first year do so because of an inability to maintain discipline in their classroom. Some colleges and teacher training programs respond to this need by offering specific courses in methods of control. Others do not! Some state legislatures require formal coursework to help teachers handle this first prerequisite to teaching. Others do not, despite the fact that learning is impossible in a chaotic classroom!

Consider the contrasting approach of the skillful teacher, Mrs. Justice. She wants the love of the class too, but she is more keenly aware of her responsibility to the students. On the first day of school she delivers her inaugural address, but it is very different from the one being spoken by Miss Peach. She says, in effect, "This is going to be a good year, and I'm glad you are my students. I want you to know that each one of you is important to me. I hope you will feel free to ask your questions, and enjoy learning in this class; I will not allow anyone to laugh at you, because it hurts to be laughed at. I will never embarrass you intentionally, and I want to be your friend. Well, we have some work to do so let's get started. Would you take out your math books and turn to page 4."

Mrs. Justice just sounds like she knows what she's doing. Nevertheless, Butch's counterpart makes himself known about three days later. (There's at least one Butch in every classroom. If the troublemaker leaves during the year, a new demagogue will rise to take his place.) He challenges Mrs. Justice in a small way, but she was not caught unprepared. She's been expecting him, and she socks it to him. He loses big! Everyone in the class gets the message: It doesn't pay to attack Mrs. J. Wow! Poor Butch didn't do so well, did he?

Mrs. Justice then delivers a little speech she has been saving for this moment. She says, "There's something each of you should know. Your parents have given me the responsibility of teaching you some very important things this year, and I intend not to disappoint them. I have to get you ready for the things you will need to know next year. That's why I can't let one or two show-offs keep me from doing my job. Now, if you want to try to interfere with that purpose and disrupt what we're here to do, I can tell you it will be a miserable year for you. I have many ways to make you uncomfortable, and I will not hesitate to use them. Any questions? Good, let's get back to work."

Mrs. Justice then proceeds to follow a little formula that I favor tongue in cheek: don't smile till Thanksgiving. By November, this competent teacher has made her point. The class knows she's tougher, wiser, and braver than they are. Here comes the good news: Then they can begin to enjoy the pleasure of this foundation. She can loosen her control; the class can laugh together, talk together, and play together. But when she says, "It is time to get back to work," they do it because they know she is capable of enforcing her leadership. She does not scream. She does not hit. In fact, she can pour out the individual affection that most children need so badly. The class responds with deep love that will never be forgotten in those thirty-two lives. Mrs. Justice has harvested the greatest source of satisfaction available in the teaching profession: awareness of profound influence on human lives.

Let me add, in conclusion, that there are tens of thousands of "Mrs. Justices" out there in public and private education today, who have put their lives on the line for their students. They should be among the most highly respected members of society because of their contribution to the development of human potential. Each of us can think back to teachers like Mrs. J. in our earlier years who inspired us with a love of learning and helped make us who we are.

There are many men and women who hold this place of honor for me. I think of Mrs. McAnally, my high school English teacher. She was tough as nails, but I loved her. I thought she was going to work me to death, but she taught me the fundamentals of grammar. She also taught me to keep my big mouth shut and listen to what I was told. In college and graduate school there were other strong professors who shaped and molded my thinking: Dr. Eddie Harwood, Dr. Paul Culbertson, Dr. C. E. Meyers, and Dr. Ken Hopkins. With the exception of Dr. Meyers who has died, all of these men are my good friends, today. I owe them an unpayable debt.

In each case, however, their contributions to my life came through the avenue of *discipline*. Formal learning is impossible without it. The boring professors who asked and received nothing from me have been forgotten. The ones I remember today are those who invested themselves in me, and wouldn't take anything less than my best in return.

Does your local school district understand this necessity for structure, respect, commitment and discipline in the classroom? If so, why don't you call your child's teacher or the principal and express your appreciation. They could use a pat on the back. Tell them you stand ready to assist in carrying out their important mission. If your school system is not so oriented, get involved to help turn the tide. Meet with parent groups. Join the PTA. Review the textbooks. Work for the election of school board members who believe in traditional values and academic excellence. Schools function best when the time-honored principles of local control—by parents—prevails. I believe it is making a comeback!

We'll pause now for a few more questions related to these unbiased and absolutely objective thoughts, and then look at a correlated aspect of discipline in learning.

QUESTIONS AND ANSWERS

Q *When Mrs. Justice told her class that she had many ways to make her rebellious students uncomfortable, I would like to know what those things are. I feel handicapped in my district. What alternatives are there, given the limitations that are now on teachers?*

A If a school district is committed to discipline and structure in the classroom, there are many things that Mrs. Justice can do when challenged. Before I suggest a couple, let me say that the strong teacher rarely has to deliver on a threat, just as a father who may be the stronger disciplinarian at home usually punishes less than the mother. There is something in the manner of a confident leader that says, "Don't push me too far." Some of it is convincing bluff. Some is in the way the first challenge is handled, as with Mrs. Justice. And some is in the teacher's ability to express love to the child. Unfortunately, these are not skills that can be easily taught or reduced to a formula in a textbook. They *can* be learned somewhat from experience and from working with a good role model.

My wife, who was a wonderful teacher and a skilled manager of children, learned a new technique from another teacher who also taught second grade in her school. This woman used an approach that was highly effective with her seven-year-olds. She spoke in very soft tones that forced them to listen very carefully in order to hear her. Somehow, she managed to infuse those thirty children with a quiet, orderly manner just by the way she led the class. Throughout the year, her room was rather like a public library where people whispered and moved quietly around the stacks. It was an impressive, God-given skill. Some have it. Some must work hard to acquire it.

Let me address the question more specifically, now, considering those situations where disruptive students are tough and determined to force a showdown. What then? Everything depends on the age of the class, of course, but let me direct my answer at, say, sixth graders. First, one must decide what is motivating the rebellious behavior. Typically, the noisy kid seeks the attention of the group. Some children had much rather be thought of as obnoxious than to be unthought of at all. For them, anonymity is unacceptable. The ideal prescription is to extinguish their attention-getting behavior and then meet their need for acceptance by less disruptive behavior. An example may help.

I worked with a giddy little sixth grader named Larry whose mouth never shut. He perpetually disrupted the tranquility of his class, setting up a constant barrage of silliness, wise remarks and horseplay. His teacher and I constructed an isolation area in a remote corner of the schoolroom; from that spot he could see nothing but the front of the room. Thereafter, Larry was sentenced to a week in the isolation booth whenever he chose to be disruptive, which effectively eliminated the supporting reinforcement. Certainly, he could still act silly behind the screen, but he could not see the effect he was having on his peers, and they could not see him. Besides this limitation, each outburst lengthened his lonely isolation.

Larry spent one entire month in relative solitude before the extinction was finalized. When he rejoined society, his teacher immediately began to reward his cooperation. He was given the high status jobs, (messengers, sergeant-at-arms, etc.) and praised for the improvement he had made. The results were remarkable.

Sometimes these kinds of in-class responses to defiance do not work. Let's admit it. *Nothing* works for every child. In those cases, I have recommended an approach called "Systematic Exclusion." The parents are asked to come for a conference and are made aware of the extreme behavioral problems that have developed. They are then informed that the only way for their child to remain in a public school is for the student, the school, and the parents to enter into a three-party contract. It must be agreed that the mother or father will come to school and pick up the child if they are called during the school day. The child is told that he can come to school each morning, but the moment he breaks one of the well-defined rules, he will be sent home. No protests will be successful. He might be ejected for pushing other pupils in the line at 9:01 A.M. Or he may make it until 1:15 or later before dismissal occurs. There are no second chances, although the child is free to return at the start of school the following morning.

Despite the common belief that children hate school, most of them hate staying home even more. Daytime television gets pretty monotonous, particularly under the hostile eye of a mom who had to interrupt her activities to come get her wayward son. Disruptive behavior is sometimes quickly extinguished under this controlled setting. It just isn't profitable for the student to challenge the system. Positive reinforcement in the form of rewards is then generously applied for the child's attempts to learn and study.

I worked with another child in a behavior modification classroom who was termed the most disruptive youngster ever seen at a major Los Angeles neuropsychiatric hospital. After four months in this controlled setting, he was able to attend a regular class in the public schools. *If* you can control the variables, you can usually influence behavior.

Finally, let me return to the first comment I made in response to your question. Everything depends on the policy of a local school district. If the board and administration are committed to discipline and structure, control *can* be achieved. The teacher is not left to do battle with a room full of energetic, giggling, blabbing troops who outnumber him or her thirty-five to one. That classroom teacher is like a policeman in a squad car. He can call for backup any time he needs it, and no one blames him if that support is required.

Every teacher needs to know the principal backs her in this way. Having been in the classroom myself, I can tell you I would not work in a district that didn't believe in discipline.

Q *You didn't mention corporal punishment as a deterrent to school misbehavior. Do you believe in spanking our students?*

A Corporal punishment is not effective at the junior and senior high school levels, and I do not recommend its application. It can be useful for elementary students, especially with amateur clowns (as opposed to hard-core professionals). I am also opposed to abolishing spanking in schools because we have systematically eliminated the tools with which teachers have traditionally backed up their word. We're down now to a precious few. Let's not go any farther in that direction.

Q *Would you provide one more example of discipline in the classroom? Teachers need every technique they can get to reinforce their leadership these days. Describe a system that has worked.*

A Here's an idea that you might try. My wife, Shirley, taught school for five years before resigning to have a baby. Several years after Danae was born, Shirley decided to substitute a few days per week to help us support my expenses in U.S.C. graduate school. The first thing she noticed when she went back to teaching was that it was much harder to control a class as a substitute than as a full-time teacher.

"Oh boy!" shouted the kids when they saw her coming. "We'll have fun today!"

Shirley and I sat down and discussed the struggles she was having with the children (grades 2–5) she encountered each day. "Loving them isn't enough," she said. "I need some leverage to keep them in order."

We put our heads together and came up with a concept we called "Magic Chalk." This is how it worked. Shirley would get to the classroom early and draw a simple skull and crossbones on the left side of the chalk board. Underneath were the words *POISON LIST*.

Beside the scary drawing she taped a single piece of paper. Then Shirley opened the doors and invited the students to come in. She did not, however, mention the skull as she pleasantly greeted her wide-eyed students. Within minutes, someone raised a hand to ask what everyone wanted to know: "What's that picture there on the board?"

"Oh yes," said Mrs. Dobson. "I meant to tell you about the Poison List."

"First," she said, "let me describe our class rules, today." She told them they would need to raise their hands before talking; to stay in their seats until given permission to leave, and to ask for help if they needed paper or to sharpen a pencil, etc.

"Now, if you forget and break one of the rules, you will be asked to write your name on the board to the left of the poison symbol. Nothing will happen if you do. *But*, if you get your name on the board and then get two more marks by it— then—(she said with ominous overtones) ... *then!* your name goes on the Poison List. All I have to say to you is ... *Don't!* get your name on the Poison List." Shirley never quite told them what would happen to those unfortunate troops who made the big, bad list, but it *sounded* terrible. She hinted that it involved the principal, but she never explained how.

Then Shirley quickly walked over to her desk where a brand-new piece of chalk sat in a cup on the edge of her desk.

"Does anyone know what this is?" she asked cheerfully.

"That's a piece of chalk," several said at once.

"Not so!" replied Mrs. Dobson. "It may look like ordinary chalk, but it is much more important than that. This is *Magic Chalk*. Believe it or not, this little white stick has the ability to hear. It has tiny little ears right there on the side. It can also see you. Tiny eyes appear right there on the end." (She had drawn them in.) "The Magic Chalk is going to sit here on the edge of my desk, watching you and listening to what you say. It is looking for someone in particular. The Magic Chalk is hoping to see a boy or girl who is working very hard and being very quiet. And if it finds a student like that, it will suddenly appear on that person's desk."

"If you are the one chosen by the Magic Chalk, you do not have to ask what to do. Just pick it up, walk to the board and write your name over at the right side. Then for everyone chosen by the last class in the afternoon, you get a special treat." (Are you ready for this?) "You will be permitted to leave school three minutes early at the end of the day!"

Big deal? You bet it was. The three-minute factor was not so important in itself, but enjoying the status of being chosen by the Chalk—writing your name on the board for all the world to see—and then walking out of class when others had to stay—it was a treasure. There was also the thrill of having the chalk show up on one's desk, while others were working for the same goal.

The system worked like a charm because the kids loved it. In nearly two years of application every time Shirley was in the classroom, she usually managed to include most boys' and girls' names on the Magic Chalk list. But in all that time, she never once got a child's name on the Poison List.

I consider this approach to have had all ingredients of a well-designed system of discipline. First, it was fun for the kids. Second, it offered something to gain for doing things right and something to lose for misbehaving. Third, it required no anger on the part of the teacher. And fourth, it was easy to implement.

Use your creativity to design a program for yourself. Elementary school students are suckers for games, fantasies, and contrived symbols or status. Junior and senior high students are remarkably tougher to entice.

Q *Did any parent or administrator complain about Shirley's use of the symbol for death, or about having the children unsupervised in the hall three minutes early? And what about associating a child with poison—a deadly substance.*

A No one ever criticized the system, to my knowledge, although they certainly *could* have. *Any* system of discipline will be opposed by some people today. Whether misbehaving children are kept after school ("The day is long enough already") or made to write sentences one hundred times ("What a waste of effort—there's no learning in it"), or if really troubled kids are suspended from school, ("Philosophically we're opposed to it") or if corporal punishment is used ("It doesn't work and is cruel"), there is no method of controlling children that won't draw fire from *someone*. I think, however, that teachers should be given a little latitude for the common good. Otherwise, chaos will reign in the classroom.

Q *Myra Wolynski said in her "Confession" article that Sand and Sea would not allow classroom organization or structure because it damaged creativity. I have heard that view expressed many times. Can it be supported?*

A We've all heard the warning that firm discipline destroys creativity, and there have been some studies to validate that assumption. However, it seems to me that creativity can flourish only when there's enough order to allow for concentrated thought. Chaos and creativity don't mix. On the other hand, an extremely oppressive atmosphere also stifles learning, which is what the research demonstrates. Everything seems to circle back to that word *balance,* which certainly has its place in the classroom.

Q *What would you do if you had an elementary school child in a chaotic classroom with a disorganized teacher?*

A I would do everything I could to reassign my child with another teacher. Some very bad habits and attitudes can develop in ten months with an incompetent role model. Home schooling or private education might be considered, if resources permitted.

Q *How do you feel about year-round schools in areas where overcrowding makes them advantageous?*

A Year-round schools are very hard on families. Siblings attending different schools may have their vacations at different times, making it impossible for families to take trips together. It is also more difficult to coordinate children's time off with parent's schedules. In short, year-round schools represent just one more hardship on families seeking to do fun and recreational things together each year.

Q *You indicated the Alternative School in Seattle had no formal curriculum, no grades, no overall program, etc. I assume, by contrast, that you favor a curriculum that emphasizes the memorization of specific facts, which I consider to be a very low level of learning. We need to teach concepts to our kids and help them learn how to think—not just fill their heads with a bunch of details.*

A I agree that we want to teach concepts to students, but that does not occur in a vacuum. For example, we would like them to understand the concept of the solar system and how the planets are positioned in rotation around the sun. How is that done? One way is for them to learn the distances between the heavenly bodies, i.e., the sun is 93 million miles from earth, but the moon is only 240,000. The concept of relative positions is then understood from the factual information. What I'm saying is that an understanding of the right factual information can and should lead to conceptual learning.

Q *But again, you're putting too much emphasis on the memorization process, which is a low academic goal.*

A The human brain is capable of storing some two billion bits of information in the course of a lifetime. There are many avenues through which that programming can occur, and memorization is one of them. Let me put it this way. If you ever have to go under a surgeon's knife, you'd better hope that physician has memorized—I said memorized—every muscle, every bone, every blood vessel, and every Boy Scout knot in the book. Your life will depend on his accessibility to factual information during the operation. Obviously, I strongly oppose the perspective held in some academic circles that says, "There's nothing we know for certain so why learn anything?" Those who feel that way have no business teaching. They are salesman with nothing to sell!

Q *Like you, I have observed that elementary and junior high school students—even high schoolers—tend to admire the more strict teachers. Why is this true?*

A Teachers who maintain order are often the most respected members of the faculty, provided they aren't mean and grouchy. One who can control a class without being oppressive is almost always loved by her students. That is true because there is safety in order. When a class is out of control, particularly at the elementary school level, the children are afraid of each other. If the teacher can't make the class behave, how can she prevent a bully from doing his thing? How can she keep the students from laughing at one of its less able members? Children are not very fair and reasonable with each other, and they feel good about having a strong teacher who is.

Second, children love justice. When someone has violated a rule, they want immediate retribution. They admire the teacher who can enforce an equitable legal system, and they find great comfort in reasonable social expectations. By contrast, the teacher who does not control her class inevitably allows crime to pay, violating something basic in the value system of children.

Third, children admire strict teachers because chaos is nerve-wracking. Screaming and hitting and wiggling are fun for about ten minutes; then the confusion begins to get tiresome and irritating.

I have smiled in amusement many times as second- and third-grade children astutely evaluated the relative disciplinary skills of their teachers. They know how a class should be conducted. I only wish all of their teachers were equally aware of this important attribute.

Q *Can you give us a guideline for how much work children should be given to do?*

A There should be a healthy balance between work and play. Many farm children of the past had daily chores that made life pretty difficult. Early in the morning and again after school they would feed the pigs, gather the eggs, milk the cows, and bring in the wood. Little time was reserved for fun, and childhood became a pretty drab experience. That was an extreme position, and I certainly don't favor its return.

However, contrast that level of responsibility with its opposite, recommended by Neill, where we shouldn't even ask our children to water the lawn or let out the cat. According to this recommendation, Junior should be allowed to lie on his overfed stomach watching six or eight hours of worthless television while his schoolwork gathers dust in the corner. Both extremes, as usual, are harmful to the child. The logical middle ground can be found by giving the child an exposure to responsibility and work, but preserving time for his play and fun. The amount of time devoted to each activity should vary with the age of the child, gradually requiring more work as he grows older.

A FINAL THOUGHT

As we conclude this discussion of discipline in learning, I would like to return to an interview published in the first edition of *Dare to Discipline*. It was originally printed in *U.S. News & World Report,* April, 1965, and featured world renowned criminologists, Professor and Mrs. Sheldon Glueck.[6] The Gluecks are most noted for their longitudinal study of juvenile delinquency and its causes. Note how prophetic their words were as they described the teens of their day and where society appeared to be moving.

❖   ❖   ❖

U.S. News: What seems to be causing delinquency to grow so fast nowadays?

Glueck: There are many causes for this. For the most part, however, what we are seeing now is a process that has been going on since the second World War.

First, you have more and more mothers going to work. Many have left their children more or less unattended, at home or on the streets. This has deprived children of the constant guidance and sense of security they need from their mothers in their early years.

Along with that change, parental attitudes toward disciplining their young have changed quite rapidly. In the home and outside, the trend has been steadily toward more permissiveness—that is, placing fewer restraints and limits on behavior.

U.S. News: How has that philosophy worked out in practice?

Glueck: Not very well, it seems, Life requires a certain amount of discipline. You need it in the classroom, you need it in the home, you need it in society at large. After all, the Ten Commandments impose a discipline. *Unless general restraints are built into the character of children, you can arrive eventually at social chaos.*

U.S. News: Are you saying that moral values are crumbling? (Author's note: This question preceded the so-called "new morality" by several years.)

Glueck: This is part of the picture. Not only parents, but others are uncertain in many cases as to what is morally right or wrong, and that makes discipline harder to enforce.

For instance, children today are being exposed to all kinds of moving pictures and books. It is difficult to decide what moving pictures and books should be censored.

In a broad sense, actually, you might feel that censorship in general is undesirable. Yet you also know that restraint must be imposed at some point—especially where children are involved. But in trying to decide at what point restraint should be imposed, it very often turns out that no restraint at all results. And it is this lack of restraint in the home and on the outside that is back of so much of our delinquency.

U.S. News: Do juvenile courts tend to be too soft on youngsters?

Glueck: Sometimes, yes, but more often there is inconsistency because judges have wide discretion; and they may rely on intuition and hunches rather than the use of predictive data which their staff could gather for them on each case.

U.S. News: Then is stern punishment a deterrent to further crime?

Glueck: Certainty of punishment is definitely a deterrent. After all, fear is a primary emotion in man. It plays an important part in his training. We have gone rather far in the other direction, in letting the child feel that he isn't going to be punished for his misdeeds.

Of course, it is wrong to rely exclusively on fear of punishment, but it is equally wrong to do away with this deterrent.

U.S. News: Can schools help in keeping children from developing into troublemakers?

Glueck: They certainly can. As we have said, there are children whose energies are not suited to long periods of sitting still and whose adventuresomeness has to be satisfied in some acceptable way.

We also think that one of the basic needs of schools, along with other elements of society, is a general recognition that rules must be observed—that, without rules, you drift into chaos and tyranny and into taking the law into your own hands. You see it not only among delinquents, but among young college students, in their demand for more and more freedom from restraints and from higher authority.

U.S. News: Do you look for crime and delinquency to grow?

Glueck: *Probably. Our own feeling is that, unless much is done to check the vicious cycles involved, we are in for a period of violence beyond anything we have yet seen.*

All you have to do is to read about the murders and assaults taking place in New York subways. Only a few years ago nobody thought of public conveyances as being unsafe. *We foresee no letup in this trend.* A delinquent child often grows up to produce delinquent children—not as a matter of heredity, but of his own unresolved conflicts which make him an ineffective parent.

Professor and Mrs. Glueck clearly anticipated the anarchy that is now rumbling through the midsection of democracy. Even they, however, might not have expected drive-by shootings, random killings, and murders over minor arguments in traffic. Isn't it time for us to address the root causes which the Gluecks recognized three decades ago?

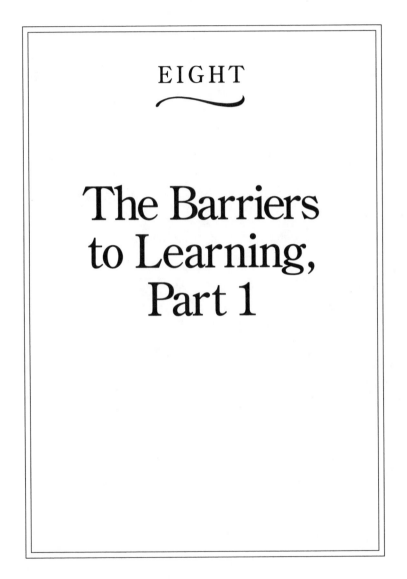

EIGHT

The Barriers
to Learning,
Part 1

W e have been discussing the importance of discipline in the parent-child relationship, particularly as concerned with obedience, respect, and responsibility. We have also examined the importance of authority in the classroom. Now it is appropriate to examine another aspect of discipline: that dealing with the training of a child's mental faculties and moral character.

The primary concern will be with the millions of children who do not succeed in school—the "academic casualties" who cannot, or will not, carry the intellectual responsibility expected of them. Their parents cry and beg and threaten; their teachers push and shove and warn. Nevertheless, they sit year after year in passive resistance to the adult coercion. Who are these youngsters for whom academic discipline seems so difficult? Are they lazy? Are they unintelligent? Do they care? Are our teaching methods ineffective? How can we help them avoid the sting of failure in these early experiences?

During my years of service as a school psychologist, I was impressed by the similarities in the students who were referred to me with learning problems. Although each child was an individual with unique characteristics, the majority of failing youngsters shared certain kinds of problems. There were several sets of circumstances which repeatedly interfered with disciplined learning in the classroom. In this chapter and the next, I will describe the three major categories of children who do poorly in school. Parents should look closely for the footprints of their own children.

THE LATE BLOOMER

Donald is five years old and will soon go to kindergarten. He is an immature little fellow who is still his mama's baby in many ways. Compared to his friends, Donald's language is childish and he lacks physical coordination. He cries three or four times a day, and other children take advantage of his innocence. A developmental psychologist or a pediatrician would verify that Donald is neither physically ill nor mentally retarded; he is merely progressing on a slower physiological timetable than most children his age.

Nevertheless, Donald's fifth birthday has arrived, and everyone knows that five-year-olds go to kindergarten. He is looking forward to school, but deep inside he is rather tense about this new challenge. He knows his mother is anxious for him to do well in school, although he doesn't really know why. His father has told him he will be a "failure" if he doesn't get a good education.

He's not certain what a failure is, but he sure doesn't want to be one. Mom and Dad are expecting something outstanding from him and he hopes he won't disappoint them. His sister Pamela is in the second grade now; she is doing well. She can read and print her letters and she knows the names of every day in the week. Donald hopes he will learn those things too.

Kindergarten proves to be tranquil for Donald. He rides the tricycle and pulls the wagon and plays with the toy clock. He prefers to play alone for long periods of time, provided his teacher, Miss Moss, is nearby. It is clear to Miss Moss that Donald is immature and unready for the first grade, and she talks to his parents about the possibility of delaying him for a year.

"Flunk kindergarten?!" says his father. "How can the kid flunk kindergarten? How can anybody flunk kindergarten?"

Miss Moss tries to explain that Donald has not failed kindergarten; he merely needs another year to develop before entering the first grade. The suggestion sends his father into a glandular upheaval.

"The kid is six years old; he should be learning to read and write. What good is it doing him to drag around that dumb wagon and ride on a stupid tricycle? Get the kid in the first grade!"

Miss Moss and her principal reluctantly comply. The following September Donald clutches his Mickey Mouse lunch pail and walks on wobbly legs to the first grade. From day one he has academic trouble, and reading seems to be his biggest source of difficulty. His new teacher, Miss Fudge, introduces the alphabet to her class, and Donald realizes that most of his friends have already learned it. He has a little catching up to do. But too quickly Miss Fudge begins teaching something new. She wants the class to learn the sounds each letter represents, and soon he is even further behind.

Before long, the class begins to read stories about interesting things. Some children can zing right along, but Donald is still working on the alphabet. Miss Fudge divides the class into three reading groups according to their initial skill. She wants to conceal the fact that one group is doing more poorly than the others, so she gives them the camouflage names of "Lions," "Tigers," and "Giraffes." Miss Fudge's motive is noble, but she fools no one. It takes students about two minutes to realize that the Giraffes are all stupid! Donald begins to worry about his lack of progress, and the gnawing thought looms that there may be something drastically wrong with him.

During the first parent-teacher conference in October, Miss Fudge tells Donald's parents about his problems in school. She describes his immaturity and his inability to concentrate or sit still in the classroom. He's out of his seat most of the day.

"Nonsense," says his father. "What the kid needs is a little drill." He insists that Donald bring home his books, allowing father and son to sit down for an extended academic exercise. But everything Donald does irritates his father. His childish mind wanders and he forgets the things he was told five minutes before. As his father's tension mounts, Donald's productivity descends. At one point, Donald's father crashes his hand down on the table and bellows, "Would you just pay attention and quit being so STUPID!" The child will never forget that knifing assessment.

Whereas Donald struggled vainly to learn during his early days in school, by November he has become disinterested and unmotivated. He looks out the window. He draws and doodles with his pencil. He whispers and plays. Since he can't read, he can neither spell, write, or do his social studies. He is uninvolved and bored, not knowing what is going on most of the time. He feels weird and inadequate.

"Please stand, Donald, and read the next paragraph," says his teacher. He stands and shifts his weight from foot to foot as he struggles to identify the first word. The girls snicker and he hears one of the boys say, "What a dummy!" The problem began as a developmental lag, but has now become an emotional time bomb and a growing hatred for school.

The tragedy is that Donald need not have suffered the humiliation of academic failure. One more year of growing and maturing would have prepared him to cope with the educational responsibilities which are now destroying him. A child's age is the *worst* possible criterion on which to determine the beginning of his school career. Six-year-old children vary tremendously in their degree of maturity. Some are precocious and wise, while others are mere babies like Donald. Furthermore, the development of boys tends to be about six months behind girls at this age. As can be seen, a slow-maturing boy who turns six right before school starts is miles behind most of his peers. This immaturity has profound social and intellectual implications.

One reason an immature child does poorly in school may be related to the absence of an organic substance called myelin. At birth, the nervous system of a body is not insulated. An infant is unable to reach out and grasp an object because the electrical command or impulse is lost on its journey from the brain to the hand. Gradually, a whitish substance (myelin) begins to coat the nerve fibers, allowing controlled muscular action to occur.

Myelinization proceeds from the head downward (cephalocaudal) and from the center of the body outward (proximodistal). In other words, a child can control the movement of his head and neck before the rest of his body. Control of the shoulder precedes the elbow, which precedes the wrist, which precedes the large muscles in the hands, which precedes small muscle coordination of the fingers.

Elementary school children are taught block letter printing before they learn cursive writing because of the delayed development of minute finger control. This development pattern is critically important to the late bloomer. Since the visual apparatus in humans is usually among the last neural mechanisms to be myelinated, the immature child may not have undergone this necessary development process by the time he is six.

A child who is extremely immature and uncoordinated may be neurologically unprepared for the intellectual tasks of reading and writing. Reading, particularly, is a highly complex neurological process. The visual stimulus must be relayed to the brain without distortion where it should be interpreted and retained in the memory. Not all six-year-olds are equipped to perform this task. Unfortunately, however, our culture permits few exceptions or deviations from the established timetable. A six-year-old must learn to read or else face the emotional consequences of failure.

The question may be asked, "Why doesn't the late bloomer catch up with his class when he matures in subsequent years?" If the problem were simply a physical phenomenon, the slow maturing child could be expected to gain on his early developing friends. However, emotional factors are invariably tangled in this difficulty.

The self-image is amazingly simple to damage but exceedingly difficult to reconstruct. Once a child begins to think he's stupid, incapable, ignorant, or foolish, the concept is not easily eliminated. If he falters in the early academic setting, he is squeezed by the viselike demands at school and expectations at home. The emotional pressure is often unresolvable. There is no rationalization he can give parents and teachers to explain his perceived failure. Nor is there a balm they can offer which will help soothe his damaged psyche. His self-concept is often wounded by this tension, and his personality will probably reflect the experience well into adult life.

The solution for late bloomers is relatively simple: instead of scheduling the child's entrance into the first grade according to his age, the optimal timetable should be determined by neurological, psychological, social, and pediatric variables. A simple screening test could identify extreme cases, such as Donald. The majority of children could begin school at six, although more flexibility would be reserved for the exceptional child.

Regardless of the school's adoption or rejection of this recommendation, I would suggest that parents of an immature kindergarten youngster have him examined for educational readiness by a child development specialist (child psychologist, pediatrician, neurologist, etc.). This procedure should be a "must" for slow-maturing boys for whom birthdays occur late in the academic year. The consequences of doing this cannot be underestimated. This simple procedure may spare your child many years of grief.

If it is determined that the child is a late bloomer, he can either repeat kindergarten or stay at home for another year or two. Despite common wisdom on this issue, kids who are home-schooled in the first few years of elementary school do not tend to be maladjusted or handicapped when they reenter formal education. Nor are they "unsocialized." If parents are willing to bring the at-home child into their world, talking to them and allowing them to go to the store, take field trips, help cook and work in the garage with dad, they do not need hour upon hour of formal desk work.[1] Research on this issue has been specific and most encouraging.[2]

What happens, then, when the time for re-entry occurs? In most cases, those home-schooled kids catch up and pass their classmates in a matter of months. They're also inclined to be leaders in years to come[3] because they haven't been bludgeoned in the early days of vulnerability. In other words, they are less peer-dependent.[4]

If that seems strange, remember that Jesus didn't go to school until He was twelve years old. That was the custom in Israel in those days. Formal classwork for the immature child, and indeed, even for the go-getter, is simply not necessary at the very young ages. I know this fact contradicts what the National Education Association would like us to believe; they recommend mandatory education for all four year olds. It is also unpopular among parents who have two-career families and need some safe, wholesome place for their children. But that effort to take children out of the home at an earlier age simply will not conform to the realities of child development.

This is why the home-schooling movement is growing by leaps and bounds. Our organization, Focus on the Family, recently polled a random sample of four thousand constituents to see what trends and opinions were evident among them. To our surprise, 13 percent were involved in home schooling. Though challenging for mothers (and fathers), this approach to the education of the next generation has been highly successful. It is especially appropriate for kids like Donald, who need some time to grow up before formal classwork begins.

At the time I first authored *Dare to Discipline,* I had never heard of home schooling. I had been taught in graduate school to believe in the value of earlier and earlier formal classroom experience. Now, I am an enthusiastic supporter of keeping kids with their parents for a longer time. Dr. Raymond Moore, author of *School Can Wait* and an early leader of the home-schooling movement, had a great influence on me in the early eighties. Admittedly, home schooling is not for everyone, but it has been highly successful for most who have tried it. I will say this: If Shirley and I had it do over, we would have home-schooled our two children, at least for the first few years!

Whether you home-school your little "Donald" or simply allow him to repeat kindergarten, I strongly recommend that he be spared academic pressure until he can get his spindly legs stabilized beneath his body.

THE SLOW LEARNER

The "slow learner" is another youngster likely to have great trouble with academic discipline, resulting from his inability to learn as quickly as his peers. Before going further, I must ask the reader to endure a brief technical explanation at this point. To understand slow learners, we must refer to the normal distribution of intelligence quotients representing the general population.

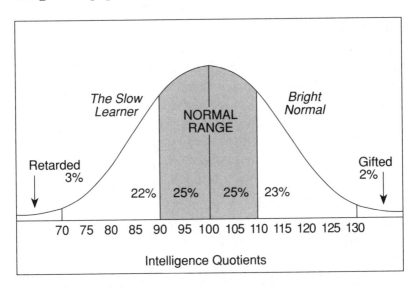

The lightly shaded area in the center of the distribution represents the "normal range" of IQ scores, which fall between 90 and 110. The precise IQ points for each category will vary according to the standard deviation of the intelligence test utilized. Fifty percent of all individuals score within this middle area on most tests of intelligence. It is interesting to note that virtually everyone thinks his IQ is above 100. If we asked ten thousand people to estimate their expected level of ability, very few would guess an IQ score below average. The fact is, half the total population would actually score below 100.

Likewise, parents will often ascribe fantastic intelligence quotients to their children. A familiar but comical remark is "Herbert has an IQ of 214, according to a test he took in the Sunday Supplement." *Very* few individuals score above 150, and Herbert is not likely to be one of them.

The "gifted" individuals are represented at the far right of the distribution. Approximately 2 percent of all children and adults have this exceptionally bright level of ability. By contrast, nearly 3 percent of the population appears at the other end of the intellectual continuum, and are referred to as "retarded." Most states provide special education for the children with intellectual deficits, and some offer an enriched program to the gifted.

As indicated, the purpose of presenting these facts is to highlight the problems of the slow learners—those children having IQs between 70 and 90. These students comprise nearly one-fourth of the children in a typical school. In many ways, they are the saddest youngsters with whom child development specialists deal. Of particular concern are the individuals with IQs in the lower range of the slow learner classification (70 to 80) who are virtually destined to have difficulties in school. No special education is available for them, *although they are not appreciably different from the borderline retarded students.*

A retarded child with an IQ of 70 would probably qualify for highly specialized and expensive educational programs, including a smaller class, specially trained teacher, audio visual aids and a "no fail" policy. By contrast, a slow learning child with an IQ of 80 would usually receive no such advantages. He must compete in regular classes against the full range of more capable students. Such competition implies winners and losers, and it is the slow learner who invariably "loses."

Let's consider the plight of the unintelligent young student in the classroom. Here is the child who "would if he could— but can't." He rarely, if ever, gets the thrill of earning a "hundred" on his spelling test. He is the last child chosen in any academic game or contest. He often has the *least* sympathy from his teachers. He is no more successful in social activities than academic pursuits, and the other children reject him openly.

Like the late bloomer, the slow learner gradually develops a crushing image of failure that distorts his self-concept and damages his ego. This was exemplified by a conversation overheard by a colleague of mine between two intellectually handicapped students. Discussing their prospects with girls, one of them said, "I do okay until they find out I'm a retard." Obviously, this child was keenly aware of his inadequacy.

There is no better way to assassinate self-confidence in our children than to place 25 percent of them in a situation where excellence is impossible to achieve, where inadequacy is the daily routine, and where inferiority is a living reality. It is not surprising that such a child is often a mischievous tormentor in the third grade, a bully in the sixth grade, a loudmouth in junior high, and a drop-out/delinquent in high school.

The slow learner is unlike the late bloomer in one major respect: time will not resolve his deficiency. He will not do better next year. In fact, he tends to get further behind as he grows older. Traditionally, the schools have retained the incapable child in the same grade level for an extra year or two, which proves to be most unworkable, unscientific, and unfortunate.

Retention accomplishes absolutely nothing but to ice the cake of failure. The accumulated scientific evidence on this issue is indisputable. Many follow-up studies have shown that children who were retained continued to fail the following year, and their academic problems were then compounded by emotional difficulties. The retained child is held back with the "little kids" while his contemporaries move on to a new grade level and a new teacher. He feels overgrown, foolish, and dumb. His relatives all know that he failed. Throughout his school life, people will ask revealing questions, such as "How come you're thirteen and only in the fifth grade?" He will reply, "Aw, I flunked third grade." It is a painful confession.

A further problem can be anticipated; the child who is retained once or twice will probably undergo sexual development (puberty) before his classmates, which can produce many unfortunate circumstances. When the slow learner finally reaches high school a year or more late, he usually finds even less tolerance for his difficulty.

One mature tenth grader was once referred to me because he announced he was dropping out of school. I asked why he was quitting, and he said, "I've been miserable since first grade. I've felt embarrassed and stupid every year. I've had to stand up and read, but I can't even understand a second grade book. You people have had your last laugh at me. I'm getting out." I told him I didn't blame him for the way he felt; his suffering was our responsibility.

Surprisingly, some unsuccessful students are still willing to struggle even after years of failure. As a psychologist, I was always encouraged when the toughest, roughest boys in high school got excited about a remedial reading program. They wanted desperately to learn this skill, but were convinced they were too dumb. This all changed when the remedial reading teacher showed them they *could* learn.

One brawny lad named Jeff was awed by his own progress. He looked up at his teacher with tears in his eyes, and said, "When I was in second grade I brought home a report card with an "F" in reading. I was sitting on the couch while my old man read it. He came over with a strap and beat the ——— out of me. Since then, this is the first time I've done anything right in school."

I was once asked to evaluate a high school boy named Willie who failed history three times. He was unable to graduate because he couldn't earn a "D" or better in this required course. I tested Willie and learned that he was a slow learner.

His teacher, who had previously required Willie to compete equally with other students, was surprised by the results. His lack of awareness of the child's limited ability seemed unfair to me, so I devised the following form letter to notify teachers of others like Willie:

Strictly Confidential

Name of Student _____

The above-named student apparently has some limitations which may be important to understanding his academic performance and classroom behavior. Although he does not qualify for *Special Education*, according to a strict interpretation of the Education Code, his intellectual ability seemingly falls into a "borderline" category. There is no legal basis for his removal from the regular classroom, but he should not be expected to compete with more capable students.

If he is required to meet an arbitrary percentage of correct examination answers, as are students with average capabilities, he must be expected to fail consistently. On the other hand, he should not be allowed to coast along without using his potential.

It seems appropriate that his grade be based on his efforts and progress, based on his individual learning capacity. To fail him in spite of his efforts is to deny him the opportunity to graduate.

I would be glad to discuss the matter with you if further information is desired.

NOTE: *Please destroy this note to minimize potential embarrassment to the student.*

Some teachers had never considered giving a slow learner an easier academic target until receiving this note. A few did not consider it *after* reading this note, either.

When I think of slow learners, the case of fourteen-year-old Robert sticks in my mind. He was five inches taller and twenty pounds heavier than the next largest student in his sixth grade class. Though retained in the second and fourth grades, Robert still had not learned to read or write. His teacher tried to motivate him every way she knew how, but Robert withstood all challenges and gimmicks. He simply quit trying.

When his teacher threatened to fail him a third time, Robert responded with horror. He could visualize himself as a seventy-three-year-old student, still sitting in a sixth grade class. That nightmarish thought motivated him to do his best in class, but his deficient academic skills prevented much progress. Robert remained in a state of anxiety until the final report cards were issued. On that morning, he was literally white around the mouth and shaking with tension until he read the pronouncement, "Promoted to the Seventh Grade."

Robert's teacher had not meant to be unkind earlier; he only wanted to obtain the best effort from this lad. Nevertheless, it was a mistake to threaten him with social disaster. A slow learner or retarded individual has the *same* emotional needs for adequacy and acceptance as a gifted or bright child, and emotional stability should not be sacrificed on the altar of education.

Despite the effects of failing a slow learner, I believe some children *do* profit from a second year in the same grade level. The best guideline for retention is this: hold back the child for whom something will be *different* next year. For example, a child who was sick for seven months in one academic year might profit from another run-through when he is well. And again, the late bloomer should be held back in kindergarten (or the first grade at the latest) to place him with youngsters of comparable development.

For the slow learner, however, nothing will be changed. If he was failing fourth grade in June, he will continue failing fourth grade in September. That's because the curricular content of each grade level is similar to the year before and the year after. The same concepts are taught year after year; the students in each grade are taken a little farther, but much of the time is spent in review.

For example, addition and subtraction are taught in the primary years, but considerable work is done on these tasks in sixth grade, too. Nouns and verbs are taught repeatedly for several years. The overlap in curricular material from grade to grade is represented more accurately in Figure A, below, than by Figure B.

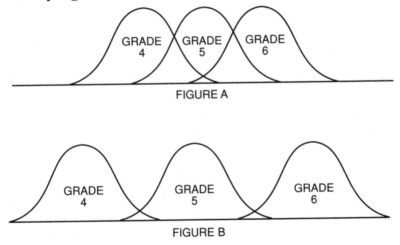

FIGURE A

FIGURE B

Thus, the most unjustifiable reason for retention is to expose the slow learner to another year with easier concepts. He will not do better the second time around! Nor is there much magic in summer school. Some parents hope that a six-week program in July and August will accomplish what was impossible in the ten months between September and June. They are often disappointed.

Since retention and summer school do not solve the problem of the slow learner, we are faced with the obvious question: What can be done for these children? Listed below are the steps that could tip the scales in favor of this vast number of youngsters:

1. *Teach them to read, even if a one-to-one teacher-student ratio is required (and it probably will be)*. Nearly every child can learn to read, but *many* children have difficulty if taught only in large groups. Their minds wander and they do not ask questions as readily. It would be expensive for the school to support additional remedial reading teachers, but no expenditure would be more helpful. Special techniques, teaching machines, and individual reinforcement can be successful in teaching this most basic skill to children who are least likely to learn without individual attention. This assistance should *not* be delayed until the fourth or fifth grades or in junior high. By then the slow learner has already endured the indignities of failure.

Many school districts have implemented creative programs to focus on reading problems. One such program, the "ungraded primary," eliminates distinctions between students in the first three grades. Instead of grouping children by age, they are combined according to reading skill. Good readers in the first, second, and third grades may occupy the same classes. Poor readers are also grouped together. This procedure takes the sting out of retention and allows slow learners to benefit from homogeneous grouping.

Another popular system is called the "split reading" program. In this method, the better half of readers in a class arrive at school thirty minutes early for specialized instructions. The slower half remains a half an hour later each day for the same purpose.

There are many such programs to teach reading more effectively. Parents who are concerned about their child's basic academic skills may wish to seek tutorial assistance to supplement these school programs.

2. *The slow learner should be shielded from the devastation of failure.* Scholastic goals which the slow learner can't attain should be de-emphasized. He should be required to do only things that are within his reach. He should be praised when he does his best, even if his work isn't on par with his peers. The slow learner is entitled to self-acceptance too, even in this fast-paced technological world.

3. *Remember that success breeds success.* The best motivation for a slow learner is to know he is succeeding. If adults in his life show confidence in him, he will more likely have confidence in himself. In fact, most humans share this characteristic. We tend to act the way we think other people "see" us.

I learned this when I joined the National Guard at twenty-two years of age. I had recently graduated from college and had already been accepted into graduate school. Thus, I enlisted for extended reserve duty in the military rather than serve two years active duty. I was immediately packed on a bus for Fort Ord, California, to undergo a six-month basic training and Army administrative course. Contrary to the recruiting posters, this exciting new career opportunity was not a matter of personal choice; it was selected for me. Nevertheless, I spent the next half year learning the fascinating world of military forms, typing, and filing. It bored me nearly out of my mind.

One hundred and eighty-three days later I returned to the local National Guard unit with this newly acquired knowledge available for usage. Surprisingly, I was not welcomed back with much enthusiasm. That's because I was a private and everyone knows privates are stupid. I was outranked by practically the whole world—so it stood to reason there was thickness between my ears. Everybody from the privates-first-class to the colonel anticipated ignorant behavior from me. To my amazement, their expectation proved accurate.

My first assignment after those months of office training was to type a simple letter in two copies. After twenty-five minutes of concentrated effort, I realized the carbon paper, used in those days, was upside down. Reverse lettering was smudged all over the back of the main copy, which did not ingratiate me with the sergeant. Similar complex procedures, like remembering regulations and procedures, were strangely difficult to perform. Looking back, it is clear that *my performance was consistent with my image.*

I then went into a tough graduate school program and earned a Ph.D. with a 3.91 grade average. Self-image was the difference.

Likewise, many children who fail in school are merely doing what they think others expect of them. Our reputation with our peers is a very influential force in our lives. This is especially true of slow learners, who represent one-quarter of all students. Perhaps your child is one of them.

In the next chapter, we'll follow the footprints of the third type of child for whom academic discipline seems so difficult. Stay tuned.

QUESTIONS AND ANSWERS

Q *If age is such a poor factor to use in determining the start of the first grade, why is it applied so universally in our country?*

A Because it is so convenient. Parents can plan for the definite beginning of school when their child turns six. School officials can survey their districts and know how many first-graders they will have the following year. If an eight-year-old moves into the district in October, the administrator knows the child belongs in second grade, and so on. The use of chronological age as a criterion for school entrance is great for everybody—except the late bloomer.

Q *What causes a child to be a slow learner?*

A There are many hereditary, environmental, and physical factors which contribute to one's intellect, and it is difficult to isolate the particular influences. Accumulating evidence seems to indicate that some slow learning and even border-line retardation are caused by a lack of intellectual stimulation in the child's very early years. There appears to be a critical period during the first three to four years when the potential for intellectual growth must be seized. There are enzyme systems in the brain that must be activated during this brief window. If the opportunity is missed, the child may never reach his capacity.

Children who grow up in deprived circumstances are more likely to be slow learners. They may not have heard adult language regularly. They have not been provided with inter-esting books and puzzles to occupy their sensory apparatus. They have not been taken to the zoo, the airport, or other exciting places. They have not received daily training and guidance from adults. This lack of stimulation may inhibit the brain from developing properly.

The effect of early stimulation on living brains has been studied in several fascinating animal experiments. In one, researchers divided litter-mate rats into two identical groups.

The first group was given maximum stimulation during the first few months of life. These rats were kept in well-lighted cages, surrounded by interesting paddle wheels and other toys. They were handled regularly and allowed to explore outside their cages. They were subjected to learning experiences and then rewarded for remembering. The second group lived the opposite kind of existence. These rats crouched in dimly lit, drab, uninteresting cages. They were not handled or stimulated in any way, and were not permitted outside their cages. Both groups were fed identical food.

At 105 days of age, all the rats were sacrificed to permit examination of their neurological apparatus. The researchers were surprised to find that the high stimulation rats had brains that differed in several important ways: (1) the cortex (the thinking part of the brain) was thicker and wider; (2) the blood supply was much more abundant; (3) the enzymes necessary for learning were more sophisticated. The researchers concluded that high stimulation experienced during the first group's early lives had resulted in more advanced and complex brains.

It is always risky to apply conclusions from animal research directly to humans, but the same kinds of changes probably occur in the brains of highly stimulated children. If parents want their children to be capable, they should begin by talking to them at length while they are still babies. Interesting mobiles and winking-blinking toys should be arranged around the crib. From then on through the toddler years, learning activities should be programmed regularly.

Of course, parents must understand the difference between stimulation and pressure. Providing books for a three-year-old is stimulating. Ridiculing and threatening him because he can't read them is pressuring. Imposing unreachable expectations can have a damaging effect on children.

If early stimulation is as important as it now appears, then the lack thereof may be a leading cause of slow learning and even mild retardation. It is imperative that parents take the time and invest their resources in their children. The necessity for providing rich, edifying experiences for young children has never been so obvious as it is today.

Q *I've read that it's possible to teach four-year-olds to read. Should I be working on this with my child?*

A If a youngster is particularly sharp and can learn to read without feeling undue adult pressure, it might be advantageous to teach him this skill. But that's a much bigger "if" than most people realize. Few parents can work with their own children without showing frustration over natural failures. It's like teaching your wife to drive: risky at best, disastrous at worst.

Besides this limitation, learning should be programmed at the age when it is most needed. Why invest unending effort in teaching a child to read when he has not yet learned to cross the street, tie his shoes, count to ten, or answer the telephone? It seems foolish to get panicky over preschool reading, as such.

The best policy is to provide your children with many interesting books and materials, read to them and answer their questions. Then let nature take its unobstructed course.

Q *Should school children be required to wear clothes which they dislike?*

A Generally not. Children are very concerned about the threat of being laughed at by their friends and will sometimes go to great lengths to avoid that possibility. Conformity is fueled by the fear of ridicule. Teens, particularly, seem to feel, "The group can't laugh at me if I am identical to them." From this perspective, it's unwise to make a child endure unnecessary social humiliation. Children should be allowed to select their own clothes, within certain limits of the budget and good taste.

Q *Do slow learners and mentally retarded children have the same needs for esteem that others have?*

A As I have explained elsewhere, I sometimes wish they didn't, but their needs are no different. During a portion of my early psychology training at Lanternman State Hospital in Pomona, California, I was impressed by the vast need for love shown by some of the most retarded patients. There were times when I would step into the door of a children's ward and forty or more severely retarded youngsters would rush toward me screaming, "Daddy! Daddy! Daddy!" They would push and shove around my legs with their arms held up, making it difficult to avoid falling. Their deep longing to be loved simply couldn't be satisfied in the group experiences of hospital life, despite the exceptionally high quality of care at Lanternman.[5]

The need for esteem has led me to favor a current trend in education, whereby borderline mentally retarded children are given special assistance *in* their regular classrooms without segregating them in special classes. The stigma of being a "retard," as they call themselves, is no less insulting for a ten-year-old than it would be for you or me.

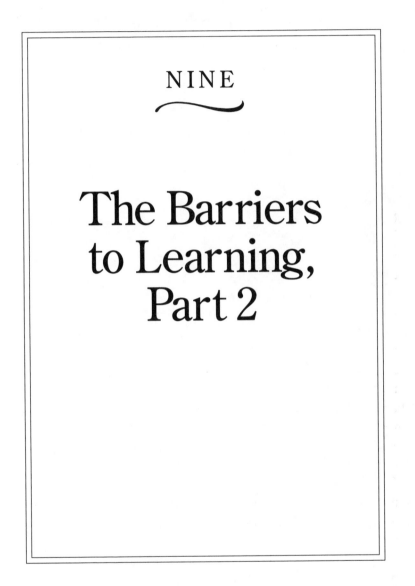

NINE

The Barriers
to Learning,
Part 2

A s we saw in the previous chapter, millions of children fall short of the standards expected of them in school, and thereby wind up as "academic casualties." These youngsters can be grouped into three general categories, including late bloomers and slow learners. In this chapter I will describe the unique characteristics of the third group:

THE UNDERACHIEVER

The underachiever is a student who is unsuccessful in school *despite* his ability to do the work. He may have an IQ of 120 or better, yet earn D's and F's on his report card. In recent years, underachievers have attained a rather high profile, thanks to Bart Simpson's self-proclaimed "UNDERACHIEVER, AND PROUD OF IT!" Despite this dubious publicity, underachievers are less understood (and more numerous) than either slow learners or late bloomers.

The apparent confusion about this group is related to the fact that *two* specific qualities are necessary to produce academic excellence, the second of which is often overlooked. First, *intellectual ability* must be there. But mental capacity is insufficient by itself. *Self-discipline* is also required. An able child may or may not have the self-control necessary to bear down day after day on something he considers painful and difficult.

Intelligence and self-discipline are frequently *not* correlated. A child often has one without the other. Occasionally, an
untalented child will struggle to achieve above his expected
level. This phenomenon is called overachievement. The opposite combination, known as underachievement, is much more
common. It is typified by the child who has considerable
intellectual potential but insists on wasting it.

It is apparent that underachievers are handled in a way that
compounds their problem. This is because, as indicated in
chapter 7, we often fail to acknowledge that learning requires
the hardest kind of effort. Examine for a moment what is
required of a high school student in a daily homework assignment. He must understand what the teacher wants, including
page numbers and other details. He must remember to bring
home the right book. He must turn off the television set and
ignore the phone in the evening. He must concentrate on the
task long enough to do it correctly. He must take the finished
product back to class the following day and turn it in. He must
remember what he learned until the next test. Lastly, he must
complete these homework assignments more than once or
twice; they must be done repeatedly throughout the year.

This kind of performance requires more than intelligence.
The fact that a child has a good vocabulary and can piece
together various manipulative puzzles does not mean he can
push himself week after week, year after year. Some children
succeed through the elementary school years, but give up
later. In fact, it has been estimated that 75 percent of all
students experience an academic slump sometime between
the seventh and the tenth grades. Despite this common occurrence, neither the school nor the home is usually prepared
to deal with it.

The typical parent reacts one of three ways to their under-
achieving child:

The first reaction is treating the problem as though it resulted from sheer stubbornness. Thus, parents may take away the bicycle for six months, ground the youngster until spring, or tear into his personhood and position in the family. Assuming the accuracy of my premise (that the behavior results from an understandable, childish lack of self-control), this reaction will not make consistent bookwork any likelier. Under these conditions, school takes on the blue hue of threat, which hardly makes the youngster more diligent.

Parents who become angry about underachievement in their child might also find studying difficult if they were suddenly thrust back in school. Resistance to mental exercise is considered natural in a mature adult but in an immature child it is assumed to reflect stubbornness.

The second approach is to offer the child a long-range bribe: a new bicycle in a couple of years or a hunting trip next fall. These delayed offers are also ineffective for reasons outlined in a previous chapter. Postponed reinforcement is tantamount to no reinforcement.

The third parental reaction is to say, "He's got to learn responsibility sometime! I can't always be there to help—so it's his problem."

If parents seem unrealistic in handling the difficulty, some schools may not be any more helpful. Teachers and counselors sometimes tell parents, "Don't worry about it. Johnny will outgrow the problem." That's the biggest falsehood of the year. Johnny usually doesn't outgrow the problem—gross underachievement in the elementary years tends to be rather persistent. Furthermore, I've observed that most underachievers are lifelong "messies." They are often sloppy and disorganized in everything they do. It is a persistent trait that goes cross-grain to what is needed in the classroom.

Over the years I have dealt with more than five hundred underachievers and have concluded that there are only two functional solutions to this syndrome. The first is certainly no panacea: Parents can become so involved in the schoolwork that the child has no choice but to do the job. This is possible only if the school takes the time to communicate assignments and progress to the parents, because Junior certainly won't carry the message! Adolescents, particularly, will confound the communication between school and home as much as possible.

In one of the high schools where I served, for example, the students had a twenty-minute homeroom experience each day. This period was used for council meetings, announcements, and related matters. Very little opportunity for studying occurred there, yet each day hundreds of parents were told that all the homework was finished during that session. The naive parents were led to believe that homeroom was a lengthy block of concentrated effort. Parents must know what goes on in school if they want to influence their child's academic responsibilities.

Also, the parents should provide *support* in areas where pure self-discipline is needed. The evening study period should be highly structured—routine hours and a minimum of interferences. The parent must know what was assigned and how the finished product should look. Ongoing research by the Center for the Study of the Family, Children, and Youth at Stanford University is finding that one method of helping the underachiever that results in a sustained improvement in grades is parental involvement. When Mom and Dad offer regular encouragement, praise for a job well done, and meaningful assistance, grades tend to go up.[1]

I must hasten to say that this can be quite difficult. Intense parental involvement can rarely be sustained for more than a week or two, because many moms and dads don't have the required self-discipline themselves. There must be a way to supplement their effort, and I believe there is.

The underachiever often thrives under a system of immediate reinforcement, as described previously. If the child is not challenged by the rewards and motivators given at school, he'll need additional incentives. These positive reinforcements should be based on definite, reachable goals. Further, the payoff should be applied to small units of behavior. Instead of rewarding the child for earning an "A" in English at the end of the semester, he should be given a dime or quarter for each math problem accurately computed.

"Bribery!" some readers will charge.

"Who cares?" is my reply, if it puts the child to work.

The use of immediate reinforcement serves the same function as a starter on a car. You can't drive very far with it, but it gets the engine going much easier than pushing. For the idealist who objects to using this extrinsic motivation, I would ask: "What alternative do we have, other than to 'let the child grow out of his problem'?"

Several examples may illustrate the specific application of reinforcement within the school setting. One of the most successful uses of this technique occurred with a classic underachiever named Billy, who was repeating second grade. His motivation had been assassinated by early failures, and he did nothing in school. Furthermore, his younger sister was also in second grade, having been promoted the same year Billy was held back. And wouldn't you know, she was an academic whiz while Billy was mired in intellectual despair.

After talking with his mother, we agreed upon a motivation system to be implemented at home. On the basis of our conference, Billy's mother quickly constructed the following chart:

For each five minutes Billy spent working on his weekly spelling words with a parent, he got to color in a bar on the chart. When all bars were colored, he would receive a new bicycle seat. He also colored a bar for each ten minutes spent

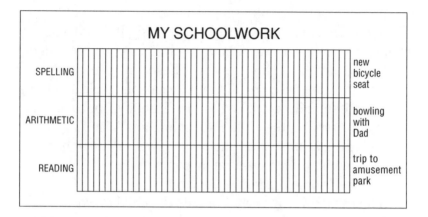

working on arithmetic flash cards. Fifty bars would earn him a bowling trip with his father. Billy's mother considered reading to be his greatest problem. Thus, reading provided the pathway to a day at the amusement park (in this case, Disneyland). As the biggest prize, it naturally took longer to earn (one bar was colored for each fifteen minutes of reading).

By staggering the reinforcement, one pleasant reward could be earned quickly, another soon after, and a grand prize waited at the end. Billy quickly caught the excitement of the game. He rushed home after school and went to work with his mother. Whereas she was previously unable to make him open a book, he suddenly wanted to "study" throughout the evening. The reinforcement system worked so well that it had an unexpected consequence. Billy's mother called me the following week to complain about not being able to get her work done when Billy was at home!

After a while, a strange thing began to happen. Billy began to learn, though that was not his intent. He spelled all his words correctly on the weekly test for the first time, and enjoyed the feeling of success that followed. When the class was discussing arithmetic he knew the answers, and waved his hand for a chance to prove his knowledge. His reading improved noticeably, and his teacher moved him out of the slow reading group. Without meaning to do so, Billy discovered the joy of learning. The vicious cycle of failure had been broken.

It would be wrong to imply that all learning problems can be eliminated as easily and successfully as Billy's. Some underachievers are "hard-core" and *nothing* will shake them loose. Yet reinforcement offers the best possibility for improvement. This system has been employed throughout the world, often with remarkable results.

In New York City, for example, it was used to help many delinquent youth who couldn't read. The young rebels, who would have laughed off a direct offer to teach them to read, had to be enticed via the back door. That's exactly what happened. Researchers told them, "Look, we've got some machines that *might* be able to teach reading, but we need your help to determine if they work. There's money involved: we'll actually pay you for each right answer." The amount of money was decent for the summer program, and most of the adolescents who accepted the offer learned to read. This, in turn, helped steer them off the street and into the classroom, thereby opening new academic challenges to them.

A similar system was applied in the Alabama prisons, whereby inmates could earn money by learning new skills and completing instructional courses. The future will bring even wider application of these principles to difficult behavioral problems, including the one of academic underachievement.

Children and adolescents, like people of all ages, want to be responsible. They want to feel the self-respect and dignity of doing what is right. The ones who fail in school are often the most miserable, but they lack the self-discipline to overcome their own inertia.

SUMMARY

In these past two chapters, I have described three great barriers to discipline in the classroom. Of course, there are additional problems which I have not presented in detail. Anything that worries or troubles a child can result in school failure. For example, deep feelings of inadequacy and inferiority can prevent academic concentration. The child who must cope with such emotions has little time for less important matters. Adults who have tried to work or think while awaiting a threatening medical report, such as a lab test for cancer, may understand this mechanism of mental interference.

Parents and teachers must never underestimate the threats a child associates with school. Regardless of whether or not he verbalizes his fears, he is often aware of many "dangers" which lurk just inside the school gate. That is, other students might laugh at him. He may be ridiculed or criticized by teachers. He could be rejected by members of the opposite sex. He may fail despite his best efforts. These and similar fears can permeate the entire world of a bewildered young student, causing him to act in ways which appear lazy. Thus, the solution to school failure often requires dealing with problems which seem unrelated to classroom work.

One further thought strikes me as very important at this point. We have discussed three categories of children, those who are late bloomers, slow learners, or underachievers. But how can a parent or teacher know if a child has one of these problems or some other intellectual deficit? The answer in a particular case can only be determined from a complete educational assessment conducted by a person trained, certified, or licensed to evaluate children. In each of the three categories I have described, a test of intelligence (IQ) is necessary to identify a child's problem. How can we know the underachiever is not a slow learner unless we measure basic intellectual skills? How can we separate the late bloomer from a child with a severe learning deficit without assessing fundamental abilities? The IQ test is an extremely valuable tool in this differentiation.

Unfortunately, IQ testing has all but disappeared in many school districts. Because these instruments (such as the WISC-R or Stanford Binet) were perceived to be unfair to minorities, their use has come under increasing criticism in recent years. Thus, it is no longer "politically correct" to use them. As a result, parents who desperately need the information previously available from testing in public school settings now have to seek out a psychologist or counselor in private practice who can conduct the evaluation. Those who lack the funds to obtain this expensive assistance, including many minorities, are deprived of the help their children need. I regret the political situation that prevents school districts from evaluating their students with the best tests available.

But what about minorities? Are standardized IQ tests unfair to African-Americans, Hispanics and Native Americans? I do not think so. It is true that minorities sometimes do more poorly on these tests because their cultures do not prepare them for that kind of exam. But read carefully, now: The same cultural factors that affect the test results also affect school performance. Performance on test questions is correlated with classroom work. If we seek a test that does not reflect the impact of an inner-city culture, then it will be useless because it will no longer *predict* classroom performance.

Let me say it once more. The purpose of testing is to estimate how well a given child is likely to do in an academic setting. To create an instrument that will not reflect the handicap his culture will place on him, when that culture will definitely handicap him in the classroom, is to play games with "political correctness."

If you didn't understand what I just wrote, please remember this. All children with learning problems, including some minorities, need to be evaluated with standardized tests of intelligence. Until that occurs, we don't know what the difficulty is and how it should be treated. I say, bring back the IQ test.

QUESTIONS AND ANSWERS

Q *It is my understanding that we forget 80 percent of everything we learn in three months' time and a higher percentage is forgotten as time passes. Why, then, should we put children through the agony of learning? Why is mental exercise needed if the effort is so inefficient?*

A Your question reflects the viewpoint of the old progressive education theorists. They wanted the school curriculum to be nothing more than "life adjustment." They placed a low priority on intellectual discipline for the reasons you mentioned. Even some college professors have adopted this "no content" philosophy, as I mentioned in a previous chapter. They reason that the material we learn today may be obsolete tomorrow, so why learn it? I strongly disagree with this approach to education. There are at least five reasons why learning is important, even if we forget much of what we're taught:

(1) As indicated earlier, teaching self-discipline is a very important component of the academic experience. Good students learn to sit for long hours, follow directions, complete assignments, and use their mental faculties. Accordingly, homework is relatively unimportant as an educational tool; it *is* a valuable instrument of discipline. Since adult life often

requires self-sacrifice, sweat, and devotion to causes, school should help shape a child's capacity to handle this future responsibility. Certainly, play is important in a child's life, too. Youngsters should not work all the time. The home and school should provide a healthy balance between discipline and play.

(2) Learning is important because we are *changed* by what we learn, even if the facts are later forgotten. No college graduate could remember everything he learned in school, yet he is a very different person for having gone to college. Learning changes values, attitudes, and concepts which don't fade in time.

(3) Even if the learned material cannot be recalled, the individual knows the facts exist and where to find them. If we asked a complicated question of an uneducated man, he would likely give a definite, unqualified response. The same question would probably be answered more cautiously by a person with an advanced degree. The latter individual would say, "Well, there are several ways to look at it. . . ." He knows the matter is more complex than it appears, even if he doesn't have the complete answer.

(4) We don't forget 100 percent of what we learn. The most important facts lodge in our permanent memory for future use. The human brain is capable of storing two billion bits of data in a lifetime; education is the process of filling that memory bank with useful information.

(5) Old learning makes new learning easier. Each mental exercise gives us more associative cues which to link future ideas and concepts.

I wish there were an easier, more efficient process for shaping human minds than the slow, painful experience of education. But I'm afraid we must depend on this old-fashioned approach until a "learning pill" is developed.

Q *Some educators have said we should eliminate report cards and academic marks. Do you think this is a good idea?*

A No, academic marks are valuable for students in the third grade or higher. They reinforce and reward the child who has achieved in school and nudge the youngster who hasn't. It is important, though, that marks be used properly. They have the power to create or destroy motivation.

Through the elementary years and in required courses of high school, a child's grades should be based on what he does with what he has. In other words, I think we should grade according to ability. A slow child should be able to succeed in school just as certainly as a gifted youngster. If he struggles and sweats to achieve, he should somehow be rewarded— even if his work falls short of an absolute standard. By the same token, gifted children should not be given "A's" just because they are smart enough to excel without working.

The primary purpose in grading should be to reward academic effort. Those who disagree should consider the alternative reflected in the following illustration: Joe is less than brilliant and knows it. In second grade, he quit trying to do well in school. However, when he reached sixth grade he was taught by a man who challenged him to do his best. He worked very hard to please this teacher, despite his problems with reading, writing, and arithmetic.

At the end of the term, Joe was still hard at work, although his writing had improved little and he was struggling with a third grade reader. What was his teacher to do with Joe's report card? If he graded the youngster in relation to his peers, he would have to fail him. If he failed him, Joe would never work again.

Since Joe had done his best, should he receive the same grade he got last year when he sat with unfocused eyes day after day? I think not. Joe should be praised for his diligence in the most obvious manner, and given at least C's on his report card. The teacher should quietly inform his parents of the bigger picture, and enlist their support in encouraging Joe's continued effort.

Any other system of grading will result in discouragement to children of lesser ability. Even sharper students usually work better when they must stretch for excellence.

One exception to the "grade on ability" policy should be implemented: college preparation courses in high school must be graded on an absolute standard. An "A" in chemistry or calculus is accepted by college admission boards as a symbol of excellence, and high school teachers must preserve that meaning. But then, Joe and his friends need not take those difficult courses.

To repeat, marks can be the teacher's most important motivational tool—provided they are used correctly. Therefore, the recommendation that schools eliminate grading is a move away from discipline in the classroom.

Q *My child has what has been called an attention deficit disorder (ADD) that makes it hard for him to do well in school. I understand his difficulty. But he brings home D's and F's in most of his classes, and I know that will limit his opportunities in life. What should be the attitude of a parent toward a child who fails year after year?*

A Obviously, tutorial assistance and special instruction should be provided, if possible. Beyond that, however, I would strongly suggest that academic achievement be de-emphasized at home for the youngster who has a demonstrated learning deficiency.

Requiring a child with ADD or dyslexia (an inability to read) to compete academically is like forcing a child with cerebral palsy to run the hundred yard dash. Imagine a mother and father standing disapprovingly at the end of the track, berating their handicapped child as he hobbles across the finish line in last place.

"Why don't you run faster, son?" his mother asks with obvious displeasure.

"I don't think you really care whether you win or lose," says his embarrassed father.

How can this lad explain that his legs will not carry him as fast as those of his peers? All he knows is that the other sprinters run past him to the cheering of the crowd. But who would expect a disabled child to win a race against healthy peers? No one, simply because his handicap is obvious. Everyone can see it.

Unfortunately, the child with a learning deficit is not so well understood. His academic failure is more difficult to understand and may be attributed to laziness, mischievousness, or deliberate defiance. Consequently, he experiences pressures to do the impossible. And one of the most serious threats to emotional health occurs when a child faces demands that he cannot satisfy.

Let me restate the preceding viewpoint in its most concise terms. I believe in academic excellence. I want to maximize every ounce of intellectual potential which a child possesses. I don't believe in letting him behave irresponsibly simply because he doesn't choose to work. Without question, there is a lasting benefit to be derived from educational discipline.

On the other hand, some things in life are more important than academic excellence, and self-esteem is one of them. A child can survive, if he must, without knowing a noun from a verb. But if he doesn't have some measure of self-confidence and personal respect, he won't have a chance in life.

I want to assert my conviction that the child who is unequipped to prosper in the traditional educational setting is not inferior to his peers. He possesses the same degree of human worth and dignity as the intellectual young superstar. It is a foolish cultural distortion that causes us to evaluate the worth of children according to the abilities and physical features they may (or may not) possess.

Every child is of equal worth in the sight of God, and that is good enough for me. Thus, if my little boy or girl can't be successful in one environment, we'll just look for another. Any loving parent would do the same.[2]

TEN

Discipline
in Morality

My friend and colleague, attorney Gary Bauer, served for eight years in the Reagan administration, ultimately being appointed Senior Domestic Policy Advisor to the President. During his latter years in the White House, Bauer also headed an historic Commission on the Family that revealed surprising findings about the nation's adolescents.

After two years of investigation, Bauer's commission learned that Americans in every age category were better-off at the time of the study than they had been ten years earlier. Both adults and younger children were found to be more healthy, better fed, and better educated than before. More tax money was being spent on children and more programs and bureaucrats were in place to address their needs. There was, however, a striking exception to this conclusion.

Teenagers were found to be considerably *worse* off than in the prior decade. Their many problems could not be blamed on government, on educators or on the medical community. Rather, Bauer and his co-workers found that young people were busily killing *themselves* at an alarming rate. It is shocking to see just how hostile the world of the young has become and how poorly they are coping with their difficulties.

Suppose the parents of yesterday could visit our time to observe the conditions that prevail among our children. They would be appalled by the problems which have become widespread (and are spreading wider) in our homes, schools and neighborhoods.

Gang violence and one-on-one crime among the young is an indescribable shame. Wandering droves of children and teens are shooting, knifing and bludgeoning each other at an unprecedented rate. Commonly, now, innocent bystanders and little children are caught in the crossfire, as bullets from automatic weapons spray once peaceful neighborhoods. It is not unusual in the large cities for ten or fifteen young people to die in a single violent weekend. Emergency units of virtually every inner city hospital are taxed to the limit trying to deal with the casualties of gang warfare now being waged. They call it "battlefield medicine." The killings are so common that many don't even get reported in the news. Only when the body count reaches record proportions do people seem alarmed by what is happening. Who would have believed in 1970 when *Dare to Discipline* was first written that this would have occurred?

Isaac Fulwood, Chief of Police in Washington, D.C., blamed the city's "love of drugs," when the homicide rate there set another record for the third straight year.[1] He could have just as easily pointed his finger at City Hall. At that same time, Mayor Marion Barry was making headlines around the country (and a mockery of law enforcement) for his conviction of cocaine possession.

"The United States is breeding a lost generation of children," proclaimed one authority, citing teen violence statistics compiled by U.S. Justice Department. These figures showed that since 1983, robberies committed by juveniles under eighteen have increased five times, murders have tripled, and rapes have doubled. The leading killer of black males aged fifteen to twenty-four is now homocide; only car accidents kill more white youths.[2]

"During every one hundred hours on our streets we lose more young men than were killed in one hundred hours of ground war in the Persian Gulf," lamented Dr. Louis Sullivan, secretary of the Department of Health and Human Services during the Bush administration. "Where are the yellow ribbons of hope and remembrance for our youth dying in the streets?"[3]

No longer is extreme violence something that happens only on television. It is a reality of daily life for many of our youth. In 1987, gifted students in a Washington, D.C., public school science class were asked how many knew somebody who'd been killed. Of the nineteen students, fourteen raised their hands. How were they killed? "Shot," said one student. "Stabbed," said another. "Shot." "Shot." "Drugs." "Shot." All of this from thirteen-year-old children.[4]

Similar findings were compiled in a study of 168 teenagers by researchers at the University of Maryland School of Medicine. When asked about their exposure to violent crime, an amazing 24 percent of these Baltimore teens had witnessed a murder; 72 percent knew someone who had been shot.[5]

Wherever one chooses to look within adolescent society, trouble is evident. A root cause for much of the unrest, of course, is the continued prevalence of alcohol and substance abuse by the young. A recent Gallup Report indicated that before graduating from high school, a staggering percentage of teenagers are hooked on mind-altering drugs of some type. Eighty-five percent experiment with alcohol. Fifty-seven percent try an illicit drug, and 35 percent get drunk at least once a month.[6] And lest those of us with Christian homes get complacent, there is not much difference between churched and unchurched families in the evidence of teen substance abuse.[7] It's enough to make a grown man or woman sick!

Indeed, there is an ache deep within my spirit over what we have allowed to happen to our kids. What is it going to take to alarm the mass of humanity that sits on the sidelines watching our kids struggle for survival? It is time for every God-fearing adult to get on our faces in repentance before the Almighty.

We have permitted this mess to occur! *We* allowed immoral television and movie producers to make their fortunes by exploiting our kids. *We* allowed their filth and their horribly violent productions to come into our homes via cable, video, CDs, and network trash. *We* stood by passively while Planned Parenthood taught our teenagers to be sexually promiscuous. *We* allowed them to invade our schools and promote an alien value system that contradicted everything we believed and loved. *We* granted profit-motivated abortionists unsupervised and unreported access to our minor daughters, while we were thinking about something else. *We*, as parents, are guilty of abandoning our children to those who would use them for their own purposes. Where in God's name have we been? How bad does it have to get before we say, enough is enough?!

At the core of these individual tragedies is a moral catastrophe that has rocked our families to their foundation. We have forgotten God and disregarded His Holy ordinances. But it is our children who have suffered and will continue to pay for our lack of stewardship and diligence.

Of all the dimensions wherein we have mishandled this younger generation, none is more disgraceful than the sexual immorality that has permeated the world in which they live. There is no more effective way to destroy the institution of the family than to undermine the sexual exclusivity on which it is based. Yet that has been accomplished, deliberately and thoughtfully by those who despised the Christian system of values. Today's "safe-sex" advocates are advancing that campaign with devastating effectiveness.

In 1991, the humanistic organization known as the Sex Information and Education Council of the United States (SIE-CUS) assembled a task force of twenty educators, social workers and health personnel who were asked to draw up a comprehensive sex education program for children and young people. They prepared a forty-page report for local officials preparing sex education curriculum, entitled *Guidelines for Comprehensive Sexuality Education*. The individual members of the task force are among the foremost molders of opinion and sexual behavior among the young. Take a look at what they advocate for those in their teen years.

- ◆ People do not choose their sexual orientation.
- ◆ The traditional gender roles about sexuality in our society are becoming more flexible.
- ◆ The telephone number of the gay and lesbian switchboard is ——.
- ◆ There does not have to be prescribed gender roles for dating partners.
- ◆ Masturbation either alone or with a partner is one way a person can enjoy and express their [sic] sexuality without risking pregnancy or an STD/HIV.
- ◆ Some people use erotic photographs, movies or literature to enhance their sexual fantasies when alone or with a partner.
- ◆ The right of a woman to have an abortion is guaranteed by the Supreme Court, although there are restrictions in some states.
- ◆ Gender role stereotypes can lead to such problems as low aspirations, low paying jobs, date rape, and stress-related illnesses.
- ◆ There is no evidence that erotic images in the arts cause inappropriate sexual behavior.
- ◆ Teenagers can get confidential testing and treatment for STD/HIV without parental consent.
- ◆ Many religions today acknowledge that human beings were created to be sexual beings, and that their sexuality is good.[8]

The task force that prepared these guidelines clearly has an agenda, including the promotion of homosexuality, abortion on demand, sexual relations among unmarried people, unrestricted access to pornography by the young, etc. How about it, parents? Is this what you want taught to *your* teenagers? I don't believe the majority of today's mothers and fathers agree with these objectives, but most don't care enough to oppose it, apparently.

Well, the organization I represent *is* concerned enough to speak out. We will do everything we can to save this generation of kids, who now face the threat of death from the dreaded HIV. We are passive no longer.

In 1992, Focus on the Family placed a full-page ad in *USA Today* to explain the *health* risks associated with the myth of safe sex. Its contents are so vital that I am including the entire statement, along with appropriate references, on the pages that follow. Please note as you read that even if morality were of no consequence, the sex liberators are creating enormous medical problems for us. Sooner or later, the epidemic of sexually transmitted diseases will expose the lies our kids have been told.

❖   ❖   ❖

In Defense of a Little Virginity
A message from Focus on the Family

The federal government has spent almost $3 billion of our taxes since 1970 to promote contraceptives and safe sex among our teenagers. Isn't it time we asked, What have we gotten for our money? These are the facts:

◆ The federal Centers for Disease Control estimate that there are now one million cases of HIV infection nationwide.[9]

◆ 1 in 100 students coming to the University of Texas health center now carries the deadly virus.[10]

- ◆ The rate of heterosexual HIV transmission has increased 44 percent since September 1989.[11]
- ◆ Sexually transmitted diseases (STDs) infect 3 million teenagers annually.[12]
- ◆ 63 percent of all STD cases occur among persons less than twenty-five years of age.[13]
- ◆ 1 million new cases of pelvic inflammatory disease occur annually.[14]
- ◆ 1.3 million new cases of gonorrhea occur annually;[15] strains of gonorrhea have developed that are resistant to penicillin.
- ◆ Syphilis is at a forty-year high, with 134,000 new infections per year.[16]
- ◆ 500,000 new cases of herpes occur annually;[17] it is estimated that 16.4 percent of the U.S. population ages fifteen to seventy-four is infected, totaling more than 25 million Americans— among certain groups, the infection rate is as high as 60 percent.[18]
- ◆ 4 million cases of chlamydia occur annually;[19] 10 to 30 percent of fifteen- to nineteen-year-olds are infected.[20]
- ◆ There are now 24 million cases of human papilloma virus (HPV), with a higher prevalence among teens.[21]

To date, over twenty different and dangerous sexually transmitted diseases are rampant among the young. Add to that the problems associated with promiscuous behavior: infertility, abortions and infected newborns. The cost of this epidemic is staggering, both in human suffering and in expense to society; yet epidemiologists tell us we've only seen the beginning.

Incredibly, the safe-sex gurus and condom promoters who got us into this mess are still determining our policy regarding adolescent sexuality. Their ideas have failed, and it is time to rethink their bankrupt policies.

How long has it been since you've heard anyone tell teenagers why it is to their advantage to remain virgins until married? The facts are being withheld from them, with tragic consequences. Unless we come to terms with the sickness that stalks a generation of Americans, teen promiscuity will continue, and millions of kids . . . thinking they are protected . . . will suffer for the rest of their lives. Many will die of AIDS.

There is only one safe way to remain healthy in the midst of a sexual revolution. It is to abstain from intercourse until marriage, and then wed and be faithful to an uninfected partner. It is a concept that was widely endorsed in society until the 1960s. Since then, a better idea has come along . . . one that now threatens the entire human family.

Inevitable questions are raised whenever abstinence is proposed. It's time we gave some clear answers:

Why, apart from moral considerations, do you think teenagers should be taught to abstain from sex until marriage?

No other approach to the epidemic of sexually transmitted diseases will work. The so-called safe-sex solution is a disaster in the making. Condoms can fail at least 15.7 percent of the time annually in preventing pregnancy.[22] They fail 36.3 percent of the time annually in preventing pregnancy among young, unmarried minority women.[23] In a study of homosexual men, the British Medical Journal reported the failure rate due to slippage and breakage to be 26 percent.[24] Given these findings, it is obvious why we have a word for people who rely on condoms as a means of birth control. We call them . . . parents.

Remembering that a woman can conceive only one or two days per month, we can only guess how high the failure rate for condoms must be in preventing disease, which can be transmitted 365 days per year! If the devices are not used properly, or if they slip just once, viruses and bacteria are exchanged and the disease process begins. One mistake after five hundred protected episodes is all it takes to contract a sexually transmitted disease. The damage is done in a single moment when rational thought is overridden by passion.

Those who would depend on so insecure a method must use it properly on every occasion, and even then a high failure rate is brought about by factors beyond their control. The young victim who is told by his elders that this little latex device is safe may not know he is risking lifelong pain and even death for so brief a window of pleasure. What a burden to place on an immature mind and body!

Then we must recognize that there are other differences between pregnancy prevention and disease prevention. HIV is one twenty-fifth the width of sperm,[25] and can pass easily through even the smallest gaps in condoms. Researchers studying surgical gloves made out of latex, the same material in condoms, found channels of 5 microns that penetrated the entire thickness of the glove.[26] HIV measures .1 microns.[27] Given these findings, what rational, informed person would trust his or her very life to such flimsy armor?

This surely explains why not one of eight hundred sexologists at a conference a few years ago raised a hand when asked if they would trust a thin rubber sheath to protect them during intercourse with a known HIV-infected person.[28] Who could blame them? They're not crazy, after all. And yet they're perfectly willing to tell our kids that safe sex is within reach and that they can sleep around with impunity.

There is only one way to protect ourselves from the deadly diseases that lie in wait. It is abstinence before marriage, then marriage and mutual fidelity for life to an uninfected partner. Anything less is potentially suicidal.

That position is simply NOT realistic today. It's an unworkable solution: Kids will NOT implement it.

Some will. Some won't. It's still the only answer. But let's talk about an unworkable solution of the first order. Since 1970, the federal government has spent nearly $3 billion to promote contraception and safe sex. This year alone, 450 million of your tax dollars will go down that drain![29] (Compared with less than $8 million for abstinence programs, which Sen. Teddy Kennedy and company have sought repeatedly to eliminate altogether.) Isn't it time we ask what we've gotten for our money? After twenty-two years and nearly $3 billion, some 58 percent of teenage girls under eighteen still did not use contraception during their first intercourse.[30] Furthermore, teenagers tend to keep having unprotected intercourse for a full year, on average, before starting any kind of contraception.[31] That is the success ratio of the experts who call abstinence unrealistic and unworkable.

Even if we spent another $50 billion to promote condom usage, most teenagers would still not use them consistently and properly. The nature of human beings and the passion of the act simply do not lend themselves to a disciplined response in young romantics.

But if you knew a teenager was going to have intercourse, wouldn't you teach him or her about proper condom usage?

No, because that approach has an unintended consequence. The process of recommending condom usage to teenagers inevitably conveys five dangerous ideas: (1) that safe sex is achievable; (2) that everybody is doing it; (3) that responsible adults expect them to do it; (4) that it's a good thing; and (5) that their peers know they know these things, breeding promiscuity. Those are very destructive messages to give our kids.

Furthermore, Planned Parenthood's own data show that the number one reason teenagers engage in intercourse is peer pressure![32] Therefore, anything we do to imply that everybody is doing it results in more . . . not fewer . . . people who give the game a try. Condom distribution programs do not reduce the number of kids exposed to disease . . . they radically increase it!

Want proof of that fact? Since the federal government began its major contraception program in 1970, unwed pregnancies have increased 87 percent among fifteen- to nineteen-year-olds.[33] Likewise, abortions among teens rose 67 percent;[34] unwed births went up 61 percent.[35] And venereal disease has infected a generation of young people. Nice job, sex counselors. Good thinking, senators and congressmen. Nice nap, America.

Having made a blunder that now threatens the human family, one would think the designers would be backtracking and apologizing for their miscalculations. Instead, they continue to lobby Congress and corporate America for more money. Given the misinformation extant on this subject, they'll probably get it.

But if you were a parent and knew that your son or daughter was having sex, wouldn't you rather he or she used a condom?

How much risk is acceptable when you're talking about your teenager's life? One study of married couples in which one partner was infected with HIV found that 17 percent of the partners using condoms for protection still caught the virus within a year and a half.[36] Telling our teens to reduce their risk to one in six (17 percent) is not much better than advocating Russian roulette. Both are fatal, eventually. The difference is that with a gun, death is quicker. Suppose your son or daughter were joining an eighteen-month skydiving club of six members. If you knew that one of their parachutes would definitely fail, would you recommend that they simply buckle the chutes tighter? Certainly not. You would say, "Please don't jump! Your life is at stake!" How could a loving parent do less?

Kids won't listen to the abstinence message. You're just wasting your breath to try to sell them a notion like that.

It is a popular myth that teenagers are incapable of understanding that it is in their best interest to save themselves until marriage. Almost 65 percent of all high school females under eighteen are virgins.[37]

A few years ago in Lexington, Ky., a youth event was held that featured no sports contest, no rock groups—just an ex-convict named Harold Morris talking about abstinence, among other subjects. The coliseum seated 18,000 people, but 26,000 teenagers showed up! Eventually, more than 2,000 stood outside the packed auditorium and listened over a hastily prepared public address system. Who says kids won't listen to this time-honored message?

Even teens who have been sexually active can choose to stop. This is often called secondary virginity, a good concept that conveys the idea that kids can start over. One young girl recently wrote Ann Landers to say she wished she had kept her virginity, signing the letter, "Sorry I didn't and wish I could take it back." As responsible adults we need to tell her that even though she can't go back, she can go forward. She can regain her self-respect and protect her health, because it's never too late to start saying no to premarital sex.

Even though the safe-sex advocates predominate in educational circles, are there no positive examples of abstinence-based programs for kids?

Thankfully, some excellent programs have been developed. Spokane-based Teen-Aid and Chicago's Southwest Parents Committee are good examples. So are Next Generation in Maryland, Choices in California, and Respect Inc. in Illinois. Other curricula such as Facing Reality; Sex Respect; Me, My World, My Future; Reasonable Reasons to Wait; Sex, Love & Choices; and F.A.C.T.S. etc. are all abstinence-themed programs to help kids make good sexual decisions.

A good curriculum for inner-city youth is Elayne Bennett's Best Friends program. This successful mentoring project helps adolescents in Washington, D.C. graduate from high school and remain abstinent. In five years, not one female has become pregnant while in the Best Friends program!

Establishing and nurturing abstinence ideas with kids, however, can be like spitting into the wind. Not because they won't listen, because most will. But pro-abstinence messages are drowned out in a sea of toxic teen-sex-is-inevitable-use-a-condom propaganda from safe-sex professionals. You place major responsibility on those who have told adolescents that sexual expression is their right as long as they do it properly. Who else has contributed to the epidemic?

The entertainment industry must certainly share the blame, including television producers. It is interesting in this context that all four networks and the cable television entities are wringing their hands about this terrible epidemic of AIDS. They profess to be very concerned about those who are infected with sexually transmitted diseases, and perhaps they are sincere. However, TV executives and movie moguls have contributed mightily to the existence of this plague. For decades, they have depicted teens and young adults climbing in and out of each other's beds like so many sexual robots. Only the nerds were shown to be chaste, and they were too stupid or ugly to find partners.

Of course, the beautiful young actors in those steamy dramas never faced any consequences for their sexual indulgence. No one ever came down with herpes, or syphilis, or chlamydia, or pelvic inflammatory disease, or infertility, or AIDS, or genital warts, or cervical cancer. No patients were ever told by a physician that there was no cure for their disease or that they would have to deal with the pain for the rest of their lives. No one ever heard that genital cancers associated with the human papilloma virus (HPV) kill more women than AIDS,[38] or that strains of gonorrhea are now resistant to penicillin.[39]

No, there was no downside. It all looked like so much fun. But what a price we are paying now for the lies we have been told.

The government has also contributed to this crisis and continues to exacerbate the problem. For example, a current brochure from the federal Centers for Disease Control and the city of New

York is entitled "Teens Have the Right" and is apparently intended to free adolescents from adult authority. Inside are the six declarations that make up a Teenagers Bill of Rights, as follows:

◆ I have the right to think for myself.
◆ I have the right to decide whether to have sex and who[m] to have it with.
◆ I have the right to use protection when I have sex.
◆ I have the right to buy and use condoms.
◆ I have the right to express myself.
◆ I have the right to ask for help if I need it.

Under this final item (the right to ask for help) is a list of organizations and phone numbers that readers are encouraged to call. The philosophy that governs several of the organizations reflects the homosexual agenda, which includes recruitment of the young and vigorous promotion of a teens right to sexual expression.

Your tax dollars at work!

Surely there are other Americans who recognize the danger now threatening a generation of our best and brightest. It is time to speak up for an old-fashioned value called virginity. Now, more than ever, virtue is a necessity.

The response was overwhelming to this advertisement and to our continued distribution of its message. More than fifty thousand letters came to our offices from enthusiastic parents, teachers, health workers and church leaders who applauded our efforts. Many have felt exactly as we, but perceived themselves to be powerless against the media and the government sponsored purveyors of propaganda. But the time has come for action. It's time to tell Congress to quit funding suicidal safe-sex programs . . . or else. It's time to teach old fashioned principles of morality to our children . . . not just because it's the only safe approach, but because it's *right*. It's in harmony with the prescription of Him who said,

"Woe to those who call evil good and good evil, who put darkness for light and light for darkness, who put bitter for sweet and sweet for bitter. . . . Therefore, as tongues of fire lick up straw and as dry grass sinks down in the flames, so their roots will decay and their flowers blow away like dust; for they have rejected the law of the Lord Almighty and spurned the word of the Holy One of Israel." (Isaiah 5:20, 24, NIV)

A FEW WORDS ABOUT SEX EDUCATION

I have devoted the remainder of this chapter to parents and teachers who believe in moral decency and want to instill responsible sexual attitudes in their children. Their task is not an easy one. The sexual urge is stronger during adolescence than in any other period of life, and there is no way to guarantee that an independent teen will choose to control it. It is impossible to shield these youth from the permissive attitudes which are prevalent today. Television brings every aspect of sexual gratification into the sanctuary of one's living room, and the details of immorality and perversion are readily available in the theater or from the neighborhood video store. Obviously, solitary confinement for a child is not the answer.

Furthermore, there is a danger that parents will make one mistake in their efforts to avoid another. While attempting to teach discipline in matters of morality, they must be careful not to inculcate unhealthy attitudes that will interfere with sexual fulfillment in future marital relations. Those who would teach this subject have the difficult responsibility of saying "sex can be wonderful" and "sex can be dangerous" in the same breath, which takes some doing.

How then can conscientious adults instill self-control in their children without generating deep emotional hang-ups or negative attitudes? Discussed below are the aspects of sex education which are critical to the achievement of this delicate assignment.

WHO SHOULD TEACH THE CHILD ABOUT SEX?

The task of forming healthy sexual attitudes and understandings in children requires considerable skill and tact, and parents are often keenly aware of their lack of preparation to do the job. However, for those parents who *are* able to handle the instructional process correctly, the responsibility should be retained in the home. There is a growing trend for all aspects of education to be taken from the hands of parents (or the role is deliberately forfeited by them). This is a mistake.

Particularly in the matter of sex education, the best approach is one that begins in early childhood and extends through the years, according to a policy of openness, frankness, and honesty. Only parents can provide this lifetime training.

The child's need for information and guidance is rarely met in one massive conversation provided by dry-mouthed, sweaty-palmed parents as their child approaches adolescence. Nor is a concentrated formal educational program outside the home the best alternative. The ideal approach is a gradual enlightenment that begins during the third or fourth year of life and culminates shortly before puberty.

Despite the desirability of sex education being handled by highly skilled parents, one must admit this is an unrealistic objective in many homes (perhaps the majority of them). Parents are often too sexually inhibited to present the subject with poise, or they may lack the necessary technical knowledge of the human body. For such families which cannot, or will not, teach their children the details of human reproduction, assistance must be sought from outside the home.

It is my strong conviction that churches believing in abstinence before marriage and in lifelong marital fidelity should step in and offer their help to families sharing that commitment. Where else will moms and dads find proponents of traditional morality in this permissive day? There is no other agency or institution likely to represent the theology of the church better than representatives of the church, itself. It is puzzling to me why so few have accepted this challenge, given the attack on biblical concepts of morality today.

A few parents who have their children in Christian schools are able to get the help they need with sex education. Even there, however, the subject is often ignored or handled inadequately. What has developed, quite obviously, is an informational vacuum that sets the stage for far-reaching programs in the public schools, beginning in some cases with kindergarten children.

One of the problems with sex education as it is currently taught in public schools is that it breaks down the natural barriers between the sexes and makes familiarity and casual sexual experimentation much more likely to occur. It also strips kids—especially girls—of their modesty to have every detail of anatomy, physiology and condom usage made explicit in co-ed situations. Then, the following Friday night when the kids are on a date and attend a sexually explicit movie or watch a hot TV program showing teenagers in bed with one another, it is just a tiny step to intercourse—whereas a hundred years ago it was an enormous decision to give up one's virginity. This familiarity also contributes to the terrible incidence of "date rape" in North America. In short, the way sex education is handled today is worse than no program at all. Look at what has happened to the incidence of teen pregnancy and abortion since it was instituted!

For those moms and dads whose kids are in public schools today, it is imperative that they investigate what is being taught in the name of sex education. You have a *right* to examine curricular materials and textbooks. You can and must talk to the teachers and principal about what they hope to communicate. Look carefully for the hidden agenda listed earlier in the SIECUS guidelines, such as pro-homosexual and lesbian behavior, the safe-sex distortion, the belief that premarital intercourse is a "right," and any suggestion that pits teenagers against their parents. Find out if a pro-abortion stance is taken, and if Planned Parenthood or similar organizations are invited into the classroom.

If these elements are there, I strongly suggest that you keep your kids out of the program. What better way is there to undermine the value system we have taught than to invest authority and leadership in a teacher who ridicules and undermines it. Not only would I not allow my youngster to participate in such a program, but I would help organize parent groups to institute an abstinence-based curriculum in the school. And if that didn't work, I'd begin campaigning for new school board members. I might even campaign for that office, myself.

WHY IS THERE SO MUCH RESISTANCE TO ABSTINENCE-BASED PROGRAMS?

Well, some educators honestly believe that "kids will be kids," so we should show them how to play the game right. I don't agree with them, but I can respect their honest difference of opinion. There are others, however, particularly those Planned Parenthood and SIECUS types who are in the business of promoting promiscuity and abortion, whom I believe have other motives. For them, something else is going on. The subject is not merely an intellectual debate about

❖   219   ❖

children and what is their best interest. No, the topic is highly inflammatory. They become incensed when the word *abstinence* is even mentioned. Have you ever wondered why?

I served on Secretary Otis Bowen's Teen Pregnancy Prevention Panel during the Reagan era. I accepted that responsibility because I thought our purpose was to prevent teen pregnancies. During our first meeting in Washington, D.C., however, I learned that fifteen of the eighteen panel members had other ideas. They were all "safe-sex" gurus, who wanted to spend millions of federal dollars distributing condoms and immoral advice to the nation's teens. I can't describe how emotional they were about this objective. In time, I began to understand a little more of the motivation propelling the community that makes a living from teen sexual irresponsibility.

I described them this way in the book I co-authored with Gary Bauer, entitled *Children at Risk*:

❖   ❖   ❖

Let's deal with the obvious question head on: Why do bureaucrats and researchers and Planned Parenthood types fight so hard to preserve adolescent promiscuity? Why do they balk at the thought of intercourse occurring only in the context of marriage? Why have they completely *removed* the door marked "Premarital Sex" for a generation of vulnerable teenagers?

Their motivation is not difficult to understand. Multiplied millions of dollars are generated each year in direct response to teenage sexual irresponsibility. Kids jumping into bed with each other is supporting entire industries of grateful adults. The abortion business alone brings in an estimated $600 million annually. Do you really believe the physicians, nurses, medical suppliers and bureaucrats who owe their livelihood to the killing of unborn babies would prefer that adolescents abstain until marriage?!

How about condom manufacturers or the producers of spermicide, "the pill," IUD's, or diaphragms? Would they want their business decimated by a sweeping wave of morality among the young?

I doubt it. Then there are the producers of antibiotics and other drugs for use in treating sexually transmitted diseases. They have a financial stake in continued promiscuity, as well.

At the top of the list of those who profit from adolescent irresponsibility, however, are those who are purportedly working to fight it! Planned Parenthood and similar organizations would simply fade away if they were ever fully successful in eliminating teen pregnancies. They currently receive an estimated $106 million in federal subsidies to carry out their mission, plus approximately $200 million in contributions from private sources. Do you *really* believe they want to kill the goose that lays those golden eggs?

Imagine how many jobs would be lost if kids quit playing musical beds with one another! This is why professionals who advise young people about sex are so emotional about the word *abstinence*. If that idea ever caught on, who would need the services of Planned Parenthood and their ilk? It's a matter of self-preservation.

To fully comprehend the danger posed by Planned Parenthood and related organizations, it is important to examine their philosophy and intent. What is their program? What do their leaders want? What would they do if given free rein? As I understand their agenda, it can be summarized in the following four-point plan:

1. *Provide "value free" guidance on sexuality to teenagers.* Heaven forbid any preference for morality or sexual responsibility being expressed.

2. *Provide unlimited quantities of contraceptives to adolescents,* dispensed aggressively from clinics located on junior and senior high campuses. In so doing, a powerful statement is made to teenagers about adult approval of premarital sexual activity.

3. *Keep parents out of the picture by every means possible.* Staff members for Planned Parenthood can then assume the parental role and communicate libertarian philosophy to teens.

4. *Provide unlimited access to free abortions for young women who become pregnant;* again, without parental involvement or permission.

Incredibly, the American and Canadian public seems to "buy" this outrageous plan, which would have brought a storm of protest from yesterday's parents. Imagine how your father or grandfather would have reacted if a school official had secretly given contracep-

tives to you or arranged a quiet abortion when you were a teenager. The entire community would have been incensed. Someone
may well have been shot! Yet today's parents have tolerated this intrusion without so much as a peep of protest. Why? What has happened to that spirit of protection for our families—that fierce
independence that bonded us together against the outside world? I
wish I knew.[40]

WHEN TO SAY WHAT

Let me offer some counsel now, to mothers and fathers
who want to handle the instruction of their own children and
are looking for a few helpful "how-tos." My hat is tipped to
them. Even in this enlightened day, the subject of sex is
charged with emotion. There are few thoughts which disturb
Mom and Dad's tranquility more than the vision of answering
all of their children's probing questions—particularly the
ones which become uncomfortably personal.

This tension was apparent in the mother of nine-year-old
Davie, after his family had recently moved into a new school
district. Davie came home from school on the first afternoon
and asked his mother point-blank: "Mom, what's sex?"

The question smacked her hard. She thought she had two
or three years before dealing with that issue and was totally
unprepared to field it now. Her racing mind concluded that
Davie's new school must be engaged in a liberal sex education
program, and she had no choice but to fill in the details. So,
she sat down with her wide-eyed son, and for forty-five minutes gave him a tension-filled harangue about the birds and
the bees and the coconut trees.

When she finished, Davie held up his enrollment card and
said, "Gee, Mom, how am I going to get all that in this little
bitty square?"

As Davie's mother discovered, there is a delicate art in knowing when to provide the younger generation with additional information about sex.

One of the most common mistakes committed by some parents and many overzealous educators is the trend toward teaching too much too soon. One parent wrote to me, for example, and said the kindergarten children in her local district were shown films of animals in the act of copulation. That is unwise and dangerous! Available evidence indicates that there are numerous hazards involved in moving too rapidly. Children can sustain a severe emotional jolt by being exposed to realities for which they are not prepared.

Furthermore, it is unwise to place the youngster on an informational timetable that will result in full sophistication too early in life. If eight-year-old children are given an advanced understanding of mature sexual behavior, it is less likely that they will wait ten or twelve years to apply this knowledge within the confines of marriage.

Another danger resulting from premature instruction involves the threat of overstimulation. Young people can be tantalized by what is taught about the exciting world of grown-up sexual experience. Childhood education should be focused on childish interests, not adult pleasures and desires. I am not implying that sex education should be delayed until childhood has passed. Rather, it seems appropriate that the amount of information youngsters are given should coincide with their social and physical requirement for that awareness.

The child's requests for information provide the best guide to readiness for sex education. Their comments reveal what the youngster thinks about and wants to know. Such questions also offer a natural vehicle for instruction. It is far better for parents to answer these questions at the moment of curiosity than to ignore or evade them, hoping to explain later. Premeditated training sessions often become lengthy, one-way conversations which make both participants uncomfortable.

Although the question-answering approach to sex education is usually superior, the technique is obviously inadequate with children who never ask for information. Some boys and girls are fascinated by sexual reproduction while others never give it a second thought. If a child is uninterested in or doesn't ask about sex, the parent is not relieved of responsibility.

Our two children were opposites at this point. Danae asked all the right (or wrong?) questions one night when she was seven years old. Her shocked mother hadn't expected to have to deal with that subject for a few more years. Shirley stalled for time and came to share the situation with me as I sat at my desk. We promptly invited Danae to sit down for a conversation. Shirley made some hot chocolate and we talked for an hour or so. It all went very smoothly.

Ryan, on the other hand, never asked questions about sex at all. We volunteered bits and pieces of the story as it seemed appropriate and comfortable, but the specific facts were more difficult to convey. Finally, I took my son on a fishing trip . . . just the two of us. Then as we sat there on the bank waiting for the trout to bite, I said, "It occurs to me, Ryan, that we have never talked much about sex . . . you know, how babies are made and all that. Maybe this would be a good time to discuss it."

Ryan sat thoughtfully for several minutes without saying anything. I wondered what he was thinking. Then he said, "What if I don't wanna know?"

I dragged my kid into the world of reproduction and sexuality, kicking and screaming, but I got him there nonetheless. That is a parental responsibility. Even when it is not easy, the job must be done. If you won't accept the assignment, someone else will . . . someone who may not share your values.

One final comment is important regarding the timing of sex education in the home. Parents should plan to end their formal instructional program about the time their child enters puberty (the time of rapid sexual development in early adolescence). Puberty usually begins between ten and thirteen for girls and between eleven and fourteen for boys. Once they enter this developmental period, they are typically embarrassed by discussions of sex with their parents. Adolescents usually resent adult intrusion during this time . . . *unless* they raise the topic themselves. In other words, this is an area where teens should invite parents into their lives.

I feel that we should respect their wish. We are given ten or twelve years to provide the proper understanding of human sexuality. After that foundation has been constructed, we largely serve as resources to whom our children can turn when the need exists.

That is *not* to say parents should abdicate their responsibility to provide guidance about issues related to sexuality, dating, marriage, etc., as opportunities present themselves. Again, sensitivity to the feelings of the teen is paramount. If he or she wishes to talk, by all means, welcome the conversation. In other cases, parental guidance may be most effective if offered *indirectly*. Trusted youth workers at church or in a club program such as Campus Life or Young Life can often break the ice when parents can't.

I'd also suggest that you arrange a subscription for your kids to magazines that provide solid Christian advice—from the perspective of a friend, rather than an authority figure. Examples include *Brio* (for girls ages twelve and up), and *Breakaway* (for boys ages twelve and up), both of which are available through Focus on the Family. For older teens in high school, I'd suggest *Campus Life* magazine.

ASSISTANCE FROM MOTHER NATURE?

One of the areas where I have changed my perspective radically since 1970 is in recommending the use of animals, especially dogs and cats, to help explain the reproductive process to children. I *still* think a demonstration of birth is enlightening and helpful, but I am now more familiar with and concerned about the overpopulation of pets and what happens to these poor creatures when they don't have homes. In Los Angeles County alone, more than 100,000 dogs are killed every year in pounds and humane societies. Other homeless animals go hungry or are crushed on our streets and highways. Their suffering is our responsibility!

Our family has adopted our last two dogs from this population of strays, and they have made wonderful pets. Little Mitzi, our present dog, was just hours away from death when we selected her at the pound. But as a life-long dog lover, I have to tell you the selection process was a difficult experience for us. There in the plastic cages were hundreds of pitiful dogs and cats in need of adoption. Most were traumatized by their circumstances, having been lost or dumped by their owners.

As we strolled down the walkway, dogs barked and thrust their paws through the wire to get our attention. Danae put her hand in one cage to pet a lonely pup, who immediately pressed his head into her palm and closed his eyes. I'm sure he did not survive the week. I'll never forget a big brown dog with a hoarse voice who was staring at the doorway when we arrived. He was looking intently at us and yet did not seem to see. Even when we stood in front of his cage, he never took his eyes off the door. Every now and then he would emit a throaty bark that seemed to end in a question mark. Danae then read the identifying card above the cage indicating how he came to be picked up. This dog had also been brought in by his owners, and he was intently watching for their return. Obviously, we were not the folks he had in mind.

Perhaps you can understand why Danae and I were looking for the most needy animal we could find. The cute, healthy puppies and kittens had a chance of being adopted, at least. We wanted to give a home to a dog that was certain to be put down. Danae finally called me on a Saturday afternoon to tell me that she had found a good candidate.

I drove to the shelter and quickly agreed with her selection. There, huddled at the back of a cage was a twelve-week-old pup in terrible condition. She was in a state of semi-starvation, having been picked up on the street a few days earlier. Her jaw had been broken, perhaps by a fierce kick, and someone had put three stitches in her lip. We learned later she had pneumonia, round worms, tape worms, and who knows what other problems. She trembled as we approached her cage, but did not rise.

I asked the attendant to let the dog out, and he handed her to me. It was an instant friendship. She nuzzled my hand and looked up as if to say, "I'm really in a mess, aren't I?" We were hooked.

We left to talk over the matter, but couldn't forget that gentle nuzzle from so helpless a creature. Danae went back and got the dog.

I wish you could see Mitzi today. She is fat, healthy and deliriously happy. When I get home at night, she romps to the front door like a buffalo in stampede. It is as though she knows we rescued her from a living death. And surprisingly, except for a crooked mouth, she looks very much like our previous dog. So Shirley and I no longer have an empty nest at home.

Forgive this diversion from our theme, but it does relate to my earlier recommendation that animals be used to teach the miracle of reproduction and birth. Now I advise parents to have their pets spayed and neutered to prevent the continued problem with overpopulation. If puppies or kittens are desired, be sure you have good homes for them before bringing them into the world.

And if you want to befriend a lonely animal who sits today in a cage just hoping you'll give him a home, head on down to the animal shelter in your area. Neither you nor your kids will ever forget it.

(To all the animal lovers out there who've been mad at me for more than two decades for what I wrote about pet reproduction in *Dare to Discipline,* is all forgiven?)

CONCLUSION

In the first chapters of this book I discussed the importance of the child's respect for his parents. His attitude toward their leadership is critical to his acceptance of their values and philosophy, including their concept of premarital sexual behavior. Likewise, the most fundamental element in teaching morality can be achieved through a healthy parent-child relationship during the early years. The obvious hope is that the adolescent will respect and appreciate his parents enough to believe what they say and accept what they recommend.

Unfortunately, however, this loyalty to parents is often an insufficient source of motivation. It is my firm conviction that children should also be taught ultimate loyalty to God. We should make it clear that the merciful God of love whom we serve is also a God of justice. If we choose to defy His moral laws we will suffer certain consequences. God's spiritual imperatives are as inflexible as His physical laws. Those who defy those physical laws will not long survive. Likewise, the willful violation of God's commandments is equally disastrous, for "the wages of sin is death." An adolescent who understands this truth is more likely to live a moral life in the midst of an immoral society.

One further comment may be relevant. Many years ago on my daughter's tenth birthday, Shirley and I gave her a small, gold key. It was attached to a chain worn around her neck, and represented the key to her heart. Through the years, she has kept her vow to give that key to one man only—the one who will share her love through the remainder of her life. You might consider a similar gift for your daughter, or a special ring for your son. These go with them when you're not there and provide a tangible reminder of the lasting, precious gift of sexual fulfillment that God intends for His children. (They can also be ordered from Focus on the Family.)

QUESTIONS AND ANSWERS

Q *Your comments about sexually transmitted disease are very unsettling to me. I have three teenagers and am afraid they don't understand how diseases are transmitted and what they can do to the body. That is a very scary subject.*

A Like you, I wonder what it will take to awaken our young people. I interviewed Dr. C. Everett Koop while he was Surgeon General of the United States in the mid-eighties. He said then, "The AIDS epidemic will soon change the behavior of everyone. When infected young people begin dying around us, others will be afraid to even kiss anyone."

That has not occurred as of this writing, even though young people are indeed dying as Dr. Koop predicted. The following article, written by reporter Kim Painter, appeared in *USA Today*, April 13, 1992:

AIDS Surging among Teens

AIDS cases among teens and young adults grew 77 percent in the past two years.

And the 9,000 cases among 13- to 24-year-olds form just the tip of an iceberg: Thousands more are likely HIV-infected; millions more are at risk, says a report by a House committee on children and families.

The report says federal prevention efforts have been inadequate. It cites evidence that teens are risking infection through sex and drug abuse:

◆ 68 percent of girls, 86 percent of boys have sex before age 20; fewer than half report condom use.

◆ 3 million teens get a sexually transmitted disease yearly.

◆ Nearly 3 percent of high school seniors have used steroids; 1.3 percent, heroin. Shared needles can spread HIV.[41]

So why have teenagers not become "afraid to even kiss anyone," as Dr. Koop predicted? Because the natural fear of the deadly HIV has been pacified by the safe-sex nonsense. We have seemingly come up with a way to have our cake and eat it, too. It'll be the first time.

Thank goodness for a few physicians who are sounding the alarm and trying to get the uncensored facts to our kids. They don't get much press, but someday they will be vindicated. One of the most vocal of these concerned doctors is my good friend, Dr. Joe McIlhaney, an obstetrician-gynecologist in private practice in Austin, Texas. His book, *Sexuality and Sexually Transmitted Diseases*, should be read by every parent and every teenager. A frequent "Focus on the Family" broadcast guest, he talked about the fallacy of "safe sex" on a recent program:

"What you hear mostly from the press is what science is going to do for people who have a sexually transmitted disease (STD), how science is going to come up with a vaccine or treatment for AIDS, how antibiotics will kill gonorrhea and chlamydia. What is not discussed is how these STDs leave women's pelvic structures scarred for life, and they end up infertile or having to do expensive procedures to get pregnant later on.

"I could name patient after patient in the twenty-two years I've been in practice where I've had to perform a hysterectomy before a woman had the children she wanted because of Pelvic Inflammatory Disease, which is caused by chlamydia and gonorrhea," he continued.

"The public announcements about 'safe sex' infuriate me, because what they're saying is that you can safely have sex outside of marriage if you use condoms, and you don't have to worry about getting an STD. The message is a lie. The failure rate of condoms is extremely high, and that's why married people don't use them."

He went on to say, "I see the victims of these failures in my office every day. These include victims of chlamydia, probably the most prevalent STD, and of human papilloma virus (HPV), which can cause a lasting irritation of the female organs, as well as cancer of the vulva, vagina and cervix. It is one of the most difficult diseases to treat, and kills more than 4800 women a year. I also see victims of herpes, which some studies indicate is present in up to 30-40 percent of single, sexually active people, as well as victims of syphilis, which is at a forty-year high."

Rather than expecting science to solve our problems, Dr. McIlhaney said a better solution involves a return to spiritual and moral guidelines that have been with us for thousands of years:

Dr. McIlhaney concluded, "The people who made my automobile know how it works best and what I need to do to avoid car problems. They tell me that in my Ford manual. Likewise, God knows how we work best, and gave us an 'owner's manual' for the human race: the Bible. In it, He tells us not to have sex until we are married; not to have sex with anybody other than the one man/one woman to whom we are married; and to stay married the rest of our lives. That's the one and only prescription for safe sex."[42]

Q *Should a child be allowed to "decide for himself" on matters related to God? Aren't we forcing our religion down children's throats when we tell them what to believe?*

A Let me answer with an illustration from nature. A little gosling (baby goose) has a peculiar characteristic that is relevant at this point. Shortly after it hatches from its shell it becomes attached, or "imprinted," to the first thing seen moving nearby. From that time forward, the gosling follows that particular object when it moves in the vicinity. Ordinarily, it becomes imprinted to the mother goose which hatched the new generation.

If she is removed, however, the gosling settles for any mobile substitute, whether alive or not. In fact, a gosling becomes imprinted most easily to a blue football bladder, dragged by on a string. A week later, the baby falls in line behind the bladder as it scoots by.

Time is the critical factor in this process. The gosling is vulnerable to imprinting for only a few seconds after hatching from the shell. If that opportunity is lost, it cannot be regained. In other words, there is a critical, brief period in the gosling's life when this instinctual learning is possible.

There is also a critical period when certain kinds of instruction are easier in the life of children. Although humans have no instincts (only drives, reflexes, urges, etc.), there is a brief period during childhood when youngsters are vulnerable to religious training. Their concepts of right and wrong are formulated during this time, and their view of God begins to solidify.

As in the case of the gosling, the opportunity of that period must be seized when it is available. Leaders of the Catholic Church have been widely quoted as saying, "Give us the child until he is seven years old and we'll have him for life." They are usually correct, because permanent attitudes can be instilled during these seven vulnerable years.

Unfortunately, however, the opposite is also true. The absence or misapplication of instruction through that prime-time period may place a severe limitation on the depth of a child's later devotion to God. When parents withhold indoctrination from their small children, allowing them to "decide for themselves," the adults are almost guaranteeing that their youngsters will "decide" in the negative. If parents want their children to have a meaningful faith, they must give up any misguided attempts at objectivity. Children listen closely to discover just how much their parents believe what they preach. Any indecision or ethical confusion from the parent is likely to be magnified in the child.

After the middle adolescent age, (ending at about fifteen years), children resent being told exactly what to believe. They don't want religion "forced down their throats," and should be given more autonomy in what they believe. If the early exposure has been properly conducted, children will have an inner mainstay to steady them. Their early indoctrination, then, is the key to the spiritual attitudes they carry into adulthood.

Q *My young daughter recently told me that she is two months pregnant. What should be my attitude to her now?*

A You cannot reverse the circumstances by being harsh or unloving at this point. Your daughter needs more understanding now than ever before, and you should give it to her if possible. Help her grope through this difficulty and avoid "I told you so" comments. Many important decisions will face her in the next few months and she will need cool, rational parents to assist in determining the best path to take. Remember, lasting love and affection often develop between people who have survived a crisis together.

Q *When do children begin to develop a sexual nature? Does this occur suddenly during puberty?*

A No, it occurs long before puberty. Perhaps the most important understanding suggested by Freud was his observation that children are not asexual. He stated that sexual gratification begins in the cradle and is first associated with feeding. Behavior during childhood is influenced considerably by sexual curiosity and interest, although the happy hormones do not take full charge until early adolescence. Thus, it is not uncommon for a four-year-old to be interested in nudity and the sexual apparatus of boys versus girls.

This is an important time in the forming of sexual attitudes. Parents should be careful not to express shock and extreme disapproval of this kind of curiosity. It is believed that many sexual problems begin as a result of inappropriate training during early childhood.

Q *Most colleges and universities permit men and women to live in coeducational dormitories, often rooming side by side. Others allow unrestricted visiting hours by members of the* *opposite sex. Do you think this promotes more healthy attitudes toward sex?*

A It certainly promotes more sex, and some people think that's healthy. The advocates of cohabitation try to tell us that young men and women can live together without doing what comes naturally. That is nonsense. The sex drive is one of the strongest forces in human nature, and Joe College is notoriously weak in suppressing it. I would prefer that supporters of coeducational dormitories admit that morality is not very important to them. If abstinence is something we value, then we should at least give it a wobbly-legged chance to survive. The sharing of collegiate bedrooms (*and* bathrooms!) hardly takes us in that direction.

Q *You have said on several occasions that a society can be no more stable than the strengths of its individual family units. More specifically, you said sexual behavior is directly linked to survival of nations. Explain how.*

A A book could be written on that topic, but let me give you a short answer to it. This linkage you referred to was first illuminated by J. D. Unwin, a British social anthropologist who spent seven years studying the births and deaths of eighty civilizations. He reported from his exhaustive research that every known culture in the world's history has followed the same sexual pattern: during its early days of existence, premarital and extramarital sexual relationships were strictly prohibited. Great creative energy was associated with this inhibition of sexual expression, causing the culture to prosper. Much later in the life of the society, its people began to rebel against the strict prohibitions, demanding the freedom to release their internal passions. As the mores weakened, the social energy abated, eventually resulting in the decay or destruction of the civilization.

Dr. Unwin stated that the energy which holds a society together is sexual in nature. When a man is devoted to one woman and one family, he is motivated to build, save, protect, plan, and prosper on their behalf. However, when his sexual interests are dispersed and generalized, his effort is invested in the gratification of sensual desires. Dr. Unwin concluded: "Any human society is free either to display great energy, or to enjoy sexual freedom; the evidence is that they cannot do both for more than one generation."

It is my belief that the weakening of America's financial position in the world and the difficulties its families and children are experiencing can be traced to our departure from traditional values and Biblical concepts of morality.

Q *Do you think religion should be taught in public schools?*

A Not as a particular doctrine or dogma. The right of parents to select their child's religious orientation must be protected and no teacher or administrator should be allowed to contradict what the child has been taught at home. On the other hand, the vast majority of Americans do profess a belief in God. I would like to see this unnamed God acknowledged in the classroom. The Supreme Court decision banning nonspecific school prayer (or even silent prayer) is an extreme measure, and I regret it. The tiny minority of children from atheistic homes could easily be protected by the school during prayerful moments.

Q *You spoke of kindness to animals. That reminds me to ask you about my seven-year-old son who is cruel to animals. We've caught him doing some pretty awful things to neighborhood dogs and cats. Of course, we punished him, but I wonder if there is anything to be more concerned about here?*

A I would consider cruelty to animals as a serious symptom to be evaluated by a professional. Children who do such things are not typically just going through a phase. It should be seen as a warning sign of a possible psychological problem that could be rather persistent. It also appears to be associated with sexual abuse in childhood. I don't want to alarm you or over-state the case, but adults committed to a life of violent crime were often cruel to animals in their childhood. This fact was verified in a recent study by the American Humane Association.[43,44] I suggest that you take your son to a psychologist or other behavioral specialist who can evaluate his mental health. And by all means, do not tolerate unkindness to animals.

Q *Is AIDS God's plague sent to punish homosexuals, lesbians and other promiscuous people?*

A I would think not, because little babies and others who bear no responsibility are suffering. But consider this: If I choose to leap off a ten-story building, I will die when my body hits the ground below. It's inevitable. But gravity was not designed by God to punish my folly. He established physical laws that can be violated only at great peril. So it is with his moral laws. They are as real and predictable as the principles that govern the physical universe. Thus, we knew (and He *certainly* knew) with the onset of the sexual revolution back in 1968 that this day of disease and promiscuity would come. It is here, and what we do with our situation will determine how much we and our children will suffer in the future.

By the way, did you know that God created the moral basis for the universe *before* he made the heavens and the earth? His concept of right and wrong were not afterthoughts that came along with the Ten Commandments. No, it was an expression of God's divine nature and was in force before "the beginning."

That's what we read in Proverbs 8:22-36, referring to the universal moral law in first person:

> The Lord brought me forth as the first of his works, before his deeds of old; I was appointed from eternity, from the beginning, before the world began. When there were no oceans, I was given birth, when there were no springs abounding with water; before the mountains were settled in place, before the hills, I was given birth, before he made the earth or its fields or any of the dust of the world. I was there when he set the heavens in place, when he marked out the horizon on the face of the deep, when he established the clouds above and fixed securely the fountains of the deep, when he gave the sea its boundary so the waters would not overstep his command, and when he marked out the foundations of the earth. Then I was the craftsman at his side. I was filled with delight day after day, rejoicing always in his presence, rejoicing in his whole world and delighting in mankind. Now then, my sons, listen to me; blessed are those who keep my ways. Listen to my instruction and be wise; do not ignore it. Blessed is the man who listens to me, watching daily at my doors, waiting at my doorway. For whoever finds me finds life and receives favor from the Lord. But whoever fails to find me harms himself; all who hate me love death (NIV).

These last two verses say it all. If we conform our behavior to God's ancient moral prescription, we are entitled to the sweet benefits of life, itself. But if we defy its clear imperatives, then death is the inevitable consequence. AIDS is only one avenue by which sickness and death befall those who play Russian roulette with God's moral law.

ELEVEN

A Moment
for Mom

A s the previous chapters have indicated, the responsibilities of effective parenthood are staggeringly heavy at times. Children place great demands on their guardians, as a colleague of mine discovered one morning when he told his three-year-old daughter good-bye.

"I have to go to work, now," he said.

"That's all right, Daddy, I'll forgive you," she tearfully replied. She was willing to overlook his insult just once, but she didn't want him to let it happen again. As this little girl demonstrated, children are terribly dependent on their parents and the task of meeting their needs is a full-time job.

Some of them are much more aware of the power struggle with their parents than Mom and Dad appear to be. That fact was illustrated numerous times after the original publication of *Dare to Discipline*. Some kids who couldn't even read knew there was stuff in that green book that helped their parents control them. One youngster went to a bookshelf, pulled this publication from among hundreds, and proceeded to throw it in the fire. Others were even more explicit about how they felt.

The mother of a very strong-willed three-year-old shared a story with me that made me smile. This youngster named Laura had managed to wind the entire family around her little finger. She was out of control and seemed to be enjoying it. Both the mother and father were exasperated in trying to deal with their little spitfire—until, that is, Mom happened to be in a bookstore and stumbled across *Dare to Discipline*. She bought a copy and soon learned, at least according to the opinion of its author, that it is appropriate under certain circumstances to spank a child. Thus, the next time Laura played her defiant games, she got a shocking surprise on her little fanny.

Laura was a very bright child and she was able to figure out where mama got that idea. Believe it or not, the mother came in the next morning and found her copy of *Dare to Discipline* floating in the toilet.

That may be the most graphic editorial comment anyone has made about my writings. I'm told Dr. Benjamin Spock is loved by millions of kids who are being raised according to his philosophy. I have an entire generation that would like to catch me in a blind alley. But I'm also convinced that some young adults who have grown up on love and discipline in balance are now raising *their* children that way. It is still true today, as it was when they were tots, that a child will be ruled by the rudder or the rock. Some things never change.

Even with a clear game plan in mind, however, raising kids properly is one of life's richest challenges. It is not uncommon for a mother, particularly, to feel overwhelmed by the complexity of her parental assignment. In many homes, she is the primary protector for each child's health, education, intellect, personality, character, and emotional stability. As such, she must serve as physician, nurse, psychologist, teacher, minister, cook and policeman. Since in many cases she is with the children longer each day than her husband, she is the chief disciplinarian and main giver of security and love.

The reality is that she and her husband will not know whether or not she is handling these matters properly until it is too late to change her methodology. Furthermore, Mom's responsibilities extend far beyond her children. She must also meet her obligations to her husband, her church, her relatives, her friends, and often times, her employer. Each of these areas demands her best effort, and the conscientious mother often finds herself racing through the day in a breathless attempt to be all things to all people.

Most healthy individuals can tolerate encircling pressures as long as each responsibility can be kept under relative control. Hard work and diligence are personally rewarding, provided anxiety and frustration are kept at a minimum. However, much greater self-control is needed when a threatening problem develops in one of the critical areas.

That is, if a child becomes very ill, marital problems erupt, or Mom is unjustly criticized in the neighborhood, then the other routine tasks become more difficult to accomplish. Certainly, there are occasions in the life of every mother when she looks in the mirror and asks, "How can I make it through this day?" The simple suggestions in the remaining portion of this book are designed to help her answer that exasperated question.

1. *Reserve some time for yourself.* It is important for a mother to put herself on the priority list, too. At least once a week she should play tennis, go bowling or shopping, stop by the gym, or simply "waste" an occasional afternoon. It is unhealthy for anyone to work all the time, and the entire family will profit from her periodic recreation.

Even more important is the protection and maintenance of romance in her marriage. A husband and wife should have a date every week or two, leaving the children at home and forgetting the day's problems for an evening. If the family's finances seemingly prohibit such activities, I suggest that other expenditures be re-examined. I believe that money spent on togetherness will yield many more benefits than an additional piece of furniture or a newer automobile. A woman finds life much more enjoyable if she knows she is the sweetheart, and not just the wife, of her husband.

2. *Don't struggle with things you can't change.* The first principle of mental health is to learn to accept the inevitable. To do otherwise is to run with the brakes on. Too many people make themselves unhappy over insignificant irritants which should be ignored. In these cases, contentment is no more stable than the weakest link in the chain of circumstances surrounding their lives. All but one of the conditions in a particular woman's life might be perfect: she has good health, a devoted husband, happy children, plenty of food, warmth and shelter, and a personal challenge. Nevertheless, she might be miserable because she doesn't like her mother-in-law. This one negative element can be allowed to overshadow all the good fortune surrounding her.

Life has enough crises in it without magnifying our troubles during good times, yet peace of mind is often surrendered for such insignificant causes. I wonder how many women are discontented today because they don't have something which either wasn't invented or wasn't fashionable just fifty years ago. Men and women should recognize that dissatisfaction with life can become nothing more than a bad habit—a costly attitude that can rob them of life's pleasures.

3. *Don't deal with big problems late at night.* Fatigue does strange things to human perception. After a hard day, the most simple tasks may appear insurmountable. All problems seem more unsolvable at night, and the decisions that are reached then may be more emotional than rational. When couples discuss finances or other family problems in the wee hours, they are asking for trouble. Their tolerance to frustration is low, often leading to fights which should never have occurred. Tension and hostility can be avoided by simply delaying important topics until morning. A good night's sleep and a rich cup of coffee can go a long way toward defusing the problem.

4. *Try making a list.* When the work load gets particularly heavy there is comfort to be found in making a list of the duties to be performed. The advantages of writing down one's responsibilities are threefold: (1) You know you won't forget anything. (2) You guarantee that the most important jobs will get done first. Thus, if you don't get finished by the end of the day, you will have at least done the items that were most critical. (3) You leave a record of accomplishments by crossing tasks off the list as they are completed.

5. *Seek divine assistance.* The concepts of marriage and parenthood were not human inventions. God, in his infinite wisdom, created and ordained the family as the basic unit of procreation and companionship. The solutions to the problems of modern parenthood can be found through the power of prayer and personal appeal to the Creator. Indeed, I believe parents should commit themselves to *daily* prayer and supplication on behalf of their children. The task is too scary on our own, and there is not enough knowledge on the books (including this one) to guarantee the outcome of our parenting duties. We desperately need divine help with the job!

The principles of discipline which I have summarized in this book can hardly be considered new ideas. Most of these recommendations were first written in the Scripture, dating back at least two thousand years to biblical times. Consider the clarity with which the following verses outline a healthy parental attitude toward children and vice versa.

> "He [the father] must have proper authority in his own household, and be able to control and command the respect of his children. (For if a man cannot rule in his own house how can he look after the Church of God?)" (1 Timothy 3:4-5, Phillips).

This verse acknowledges the fact that respect must be "commanded." It is not a by-product of human nature, but it is inherently related to control and discipline.

> "My son, do not regard lightly the discipline of the Lord, nor lose courage when you are punished by him. For the Lord disciplines him whom he loves [Note: Discipline and love work hand and hand; one is a function of the other.] and chastises every son whom he receives. It is for discipline that you have to endure. God is treating you as sons; for what son is there whom the father does not discipline? If you are left without discipline, in which all have participated, then you are illegitimate children and not sons. Besides this, we have had earthly fathers to discipline us and we respected them. . . . [Note: The relationship between discipline and respect was recognized more than two thousand years ago.] For the moment all discipline seems painful rather than pleasant; later it yields the peaceful fruit of righteousness to those who have been trained by it." (Hebrews 12:5-9, 11, RSV)

The purpose of this Scripture is to demonstrate that the parent's relationship with his child should be modeled after God's relationship with man. In its ultimate beauty, that interaction is characterized by abundant love—a love unparalleled in tenderness and mercy. This same love leads the benevolent father to guide, correct, and even bring some pain to the child when it is necessary for his eventual good. I find it difficult to comprehend how this message has been so thoroughly misunderstood during the past twenty years.

"Children, the right thing for you to do is to obey your parents as those whom God has set over you. The first commandment to contain a promise was: 'Honor thy father and thy mother that it may be well with thee, and that thou mayest live long on the earth.' Fathers, don't over-correct your children or make it difficult for them to obey the commandment. Bring them up with Christian teaching in Christian discipline." (Ephesians 6:1-4, Phillips)

"Foolishness is bound in the heart of a child; but the rod of correction shall drive it far from him." (Proverbs 22:15, KJV)

This recommendation has troubled some people, leading them to claim that the "rod" was not a paddle, but a measuring stick with which to evaluate the child. The following passage was included expressly for those who were confused on that point.

"Withhold not correction from the child; for if thou beatest him with the rod, he shall not die. Thou shalt beat him with the rod, and shalt deliver his soul from hell." (Proverbs 23:13-14, KJV)

Certainly, if the "rod" is a measuring stick, you now know what to do with it? (Note: Please don't grill me on this. I would ask that you heed all of my disclaimers related to child abuse, which I expressed in earlier chapters—especially on pages 11-12.)

"He that spareth his rod hateth his son; but he that loveth him chasteneth him betimes." (Proverbs 13:24, KJV)

"The rod and reproof give wisdom; but a child left to himself bringeth his mother to shame." (Proverbs 29:15, KJV)

"Correct thy son, and he shall give thee rest; yea, he shall give delight unto thy soul." (Proverbs 29:17, KJV)

From Genesis to Revelation, there is consistent foundation on which to build an effective philosophy of parent-child relationships. It is my belief that we have departed from the standard which was clearly outlined in both the Old and New Testaments, and that deviation is costing us a heavy toll in the form of social turmoil. Self-control, human kindness, respect, and peacefulness can again be manifest in America if we will *dare to discipline* in our homes and schools.

Let me leave you, now, with a wonderful old poem written by Alice Pearson. It focuses on *the* most vital responsibility in parenting—that of introducing our children to Jesus Christ and getting them safely through this dangerous and turbulent world. That should be, after all, the ultimate goal for every believing parent the world over.

Are All the Children In?

I think oftimes as night draws nigh,
Of an old house on the hill,
And of a yard all wide
And blossom-starred
Where the children played at will.
And when the night at last came down
Hushing the merry din,
Mother would look around and ask,
"Are all the children in?"

Oh, it's many and many a year since then,

And the old house on the hill
No longer echoes to childish feet,
And the yard is still, so still.
But I see it all as the shadows creep,
And though many the years have been since then,
I can hear mother ask,
"Are all the children in?"

I wonder if when the shadows fall
On the last short earthly day;
When we say goodbye to the world outside
All tired with our childish play;
When we step out into the other land
Where mother so long has been,
Will we hear her ask,
Just as of old,
"Are all the children in?"[1]

Appendix

A Quick Survey of Drugs and Substance Abuse for Parents

T here is no more certain destroyer of self-discipline and self-control than the abusive use of drugs. Teens who have begun taking drugs, in whatever form, often show a sudden disinterest in everything that formerly challenged them. Their school work is ignored and hobbies are forgotten. Their personal appearance often becomes sloppy. They refuse to carry responsibility and avoid activities that require effort. Their relationship with parents deteriorates rapidly, and they suddenly terminate many of their lifelong friendships. Young drug users are clearly marching to a new set of drums—and disaster often awaits them at the end of the trail.

To help parents recognize and understand a possible drug problem in their sons and daughters, we have provided the following overview of the basics. I pray that neither you, nor they, will ever need it. Though some of the facts are technical, I recommend that you carefully study and even memorize the important details from this summary, and review the glossary of drug-world slang later in this chapter. I am indebted to several law enforcement agencies and other sources for their help in compiling this information.[1]

WHAT ARE THE SYMPTOMS OF DRUG ABUSE?

At the beginning of this appendix I mentioned several of the attitudinal and behavioral characteristics of individuals who use harmful drugs. Listed below are eight related physical and emotional symptoms that may indicate drug abuse by your child.

1. Inflammation of the eyelids and nose is common. The pupils of the eyes are either very wide or very small, depending on the kind of drugs used.

2. Extremes of energy may be represented. The individual may be sluggish, gloomy, and withdrawn . . . or loud, hysterical, and jumpy.

3. The appetite is extreme—either very great or very poor. Weight loss may occur.

4. The personality suddenly changes. The individual may become irritable, inattentive, and confused . . . or aggressive, suspicious, and explosive.

5. Body and breath odor is often bad. Cleanliness may be ignored.

6. The digestive system may be upset—diarrhea, nausea, and vomiting may occur. Headaches and double vision are also common. Other signs of physical deterioration may include change in skin tone and body stance.

7. With intravenous drug users, needle marks on the body, usually appearing on the arms, are an important symptom. These punctures sometimes get infected and appear as sores and boils.

8. Moral values often crumble and are replaced by new, outlandish ideas and values. Each drug produces its own unique symptoms. Thus, the above list is not specific to a particular substance. Parents who suspect their child is using dangerous drugs (including alcohol and tobacco) should contact their family physician immediately.

WHERE ARE THE DRUGS OBTAINED?

Illicit drugs are surprisingly easy to obtain by adolescents. The family medicine cabinet usually offers a handy stockpile of prescription drugs, cough medicines, tranquilizers, sleeping pills, reducing aids, and pain killers. Paint thinner, glue, and other toxic materials in the garage are also liable to be used as a means of getting high. Furthermore, a physician can be tricked into prescribing the desired drugs. A reasonably intelligent person can learn from a medical text the symptoms of diseases which are usually treated with the drug he wants.

Prescriptions can also be forged and passed at local pharmacies. Some drugs reach the street market after having been stolen from pharmacies, doctor's offices or manufacturer's warehouses. However, the vast majority of drugs are smuggled into this country. Surprisingly, many of them are first manufactured here and sold abroad before finding their way back as contraband.

HOW MUCH DO DRUGS COST?

Though the prices of various illicit drugs vary a great deal from area to area and dealer to dealer, depending on quantity and quality, the following figures represent the approximate black market values for the substances indicated at the present time:

1. Amphetamines: $1 and up per pill.
2. Methamphetamine: $10 per injection or snort. It is widely available in both powder and "ice" formulations, and typically sold in small plastic bags containing about a quarter-gram of the drug. Many people call it the "poor man's cocaine."
3. Barbiturates: $1 and up per pill.

4. Marijuana cigarettes: $2.50 and up for each. Marijuana is commonly sold in small plastic bags for $10 (enough for three to four cigarettes). Due to advanced growing techniques, today's marijuana is about three times as strong as what was available to the Woodstock generation during the '60s and '70s. By the pound, cheap homegrown marijuana sells for approximately $250. The same amount of a more potent, better grade marijuana can sell for anywhere between $1,300 and $3,000.

5. Heroin: $10 to $25 per injection. It is often packaged for sale in small kiddy balloons for $30 and up (enough for three "hits"). A pound, with an average street purity of 10%, costs $20,000 to $25,000. Heroin is still as popular today as it ever has been, though cocaine and marijuana currently seem to attract more attention in the media.

6. Cocaine: $5 to $20 per usage, whether in powder (for snorting) or hardened "rock"/"crack" format (for smoking). Commonly sold on the street in plastic bags for about $25 and up per quarter-gram (enough for two to four "hits"). A kilo of cocaine (about 2.2 pounds) typically sells for between $17,500 to $28,000, but can soar as high as $40,000 depending on supply. A pound, with a typical street purity of 55%-65%, costs between $12,000 to $16,000. The sale of this drug is truly big business.

7. Hallucinogens: $1 to $10 per usage, though prices vary considerably depending on the quality and type. These days, LSD (acid) typically sells on blotter paper imprinted with colorful decals of cartoon characters, cars, etc., and is frequently referred to by the decal. Thus, if the picture on the blotter paper were of Mickey Mouse, it would be called "Mickey Mouse Acid." LSD also comes as a liquid and as a gelatin

substance. Figure $100 to $300 for a hundred hits. Another common hallucinogen, Phencyclidine (PCP), is widely available in liquid form at about $150 to $250 per ounce, but costs about $1,000 per ounce in powder or crystal formulations. PCP is often used to lace other drugs, especially marijuana and cocaine.

WHAT ARE THE MOST COMMON ILLICIT DRUGS?

Dangerous drugs can be categorized into the five major divisions appearing below. Fundamental details are also presented to allow parents to learn what their teen probably knows already.

1. *Stimulants:* (Uppers) These drugs excite the user, inducing talkativeness, restlessness, and over-stimulation. They are commonly called pep pills.

  a. Specific drugs
- (1) Benzedrine (Bennies, whites, etc.)
- (2) Dexedrine (dexies, hearts, etc.)
- (3) Methamphetamine (speed, meth run, crystal meth, etc.)

  b. Psychological and physiological effects of abusive use
- (1) Insomnia
- (2) Loss of appetite
- (3) Dry mouth
- (4) Vomiting
- (5) Diarrhea
- (6) Nausea
- (7) Inhibitions released
- (8) Blurred vision
- (9) Aggressiveness
- (10) Hallucinations and confusion

2. *Depressants:* (Barbiturates, Downers: These drugs are used in medicine to relax and induce sleep in the patient. They are commonly called sleeping pills

  a. Specific drugs

    (1) Seconal (red, red devils, pinkies, pink ladies, etc.)

    (2) Nembutal (yellows, yellow jackets, etc.)

    (3) Tuinal (rainbows, double trouble, etc.)

    (4) Amytal (blues, blue heavens, etc.)

  b. Psychological and physiological effects of abusive use

    (1) Drowsy confusion and an inability to think clearly

    (2) Lack of coordination

    (3) Lethargic speech

    (4) Defective judgment

    (5) Tremors

    (6) Involuntary movement of the eyes

    (7) Hostility

    (8) More deaths are caused by overdoses of barbiturates than any other drug—often occurring accidentally.

3. *Hallucinogens:* These drugs are capable of provoking changes in sensation, thinking, self-awareness, and emotion.

  a. Specific drug

    (1) Lysergic acid diethylamide tartrate (LSD-25, LSD, acid, Vitamin A, etc.)

    (2) Psilocybin/Psilocyn (Magic mushrooms, shrooms, etc.)

    (3) Peyote (Mescaline)

    (4) Phencyclidine (PCP, Sherms, Lovely, Dusters, etc.)

  b. Psychological and physiological effects

    (1) Bizarre psychic experiences with heightened sensitivity to color and other stimuli.

(2) Psychotic illness occasionally occurs.

(3) Chromosomal breakage may develop.

(4) The psychic phenomena occasionally recur weeks after the last dosage is taken.

(5) Alterations in time and space perception occur.

(6) Illusions and hallucinations are experienced.

4. *Marijuana*: (Grass, pot, joint, weed, etc.) Marijuana is usually rolled into cigarettes. When smoked, the initial effect is that of a stimulant. However, continued usage will produce drowsiness and unconsciousness. Thus, marijuana is technically classified as a sedative.

 a. Psychological and physiological effects

(1) Pupils of the eye become dilated; the white part becomes bloodshot.

(2) A loss of time and space orientation

(3) Muscle tremors

(4) Accelerated pulse and heartbeat

(5) Apparent dizziness

(6) Odd behavior

(7) Loss of inhibitions

(8) Delusions

(9) User becomes "psychologically dependent" on marijuana.

5. *Narcotics*: These drugs relieve pain and induce sleep.

 a. Specific drug

(1) Heroin (horse, H, Harry, smack, brown, etc.) Heroin is an opiate. It is processed from morphine but it is much stronger. The tolerance for this drug builds up faster than any other opiate and it is therefore more dangerous. Heroin is the most dev-

astating and enslaving drug in existence. It is not even used medically in America.

b. Psychological and physiological effects

(1) Heroin is a cerebral, spinal, and respiratory depressant.

(2) The initial reaction is one of euphoria and comfort. This feeling disappears quickly, requiring a larger dose on the next occasion.

(3) Immediately after injecting heroin, the user becomes drowsy. This is called "going on the nod" or "nodding."

(4) Pupils of the eyes contract tightly.

GLOSSARY OF DRUG-WORLD SLANG

The following list will help you identify today's common drug-world slang, but keep in mind that the terminology varies in different parts of the country and changes extremely rapidly. Also, with the prevalence of wire taps and electronic surveillance techniques used in drug enforcement, users often call drugs by anything but what you see on the list. For example, an individual who wants to buy, say a couple of pounds of marijuana, from his usual source might use the word taco, banana, radio, shirt, telephone or some other nonsense word instead of the more usual grass, pot, weed, etc. Thus, if you were to hear their conversation, it might go something like this:

"I'm looking to cop a couple bananas."

"I've got one banana now, and can clean another banana and a half by Saturday."

As it is said, a rose by any other name smells just as sweet. Likewise, drugs by any other name are just as dangerous. Don't be fooled.

Having said that, let's open the dictionary to the drug world:

Acid . . . . Lysergic Acid Diethylamide (LSD-25) (Also: LSD, Paper Acid, Blotter, Blots, Tabs, Window Pane, Green Star, Sugar Cube, Blotter, White Lightning, Microdot, Acid Green, Red Green, Blue Heaven, Vitamin A, "AC", Cid, Fry)

Acid Heads . . . . Users of LSD

Bindle . . . . Small packet of narcotics (Also: Nickel Bag, Dime Bag, Quarter Bag)

Blue-Velvet . . . . Combination of a paregoric (upper) with an antihistamine

Booze . . . . Alcohol (Also: Brew, Juice, Suds, Liquid Gold, Sauce)

Bunk . . . . Poor quality narcotics

Caviar and Champagne . . Combination of rock or crack cocaine with marijuana

Clean . . . . To prepare marijuana for street sale (Also: Cut, Manicure)

Coke . . . . Cocaine (Also: Blow, Flake, Crack, Rock, Kibble Bits, Lines, Snow, Cola, Powder, Dove, C, Lady, Freebase, Toot, Baseball, Base, Girl, Doing A Line, Snorting, Dynamite, 8-Ball, White)

Dime Bag . . . . $10 purchase of drugs

Dope . . . . Drugs (Also: Junk, Stuff)

Downers . . . . A Sedative-hypnotic (Barbiturates, tranquilizers, methaqualone, depressants) (Also: Barbs, Valium, Candy, Amytal, Blue Devils, Blue Heaven, Blues, Double Trouble, Tuinal, Rainbows, Pinks, Red Devils, Reds, Seconal, Yellows, Yellow Jacket, Nembutal, Qs, Roaches, Ludes, Tooies, On Downs, Doriden, Quaaludes, Librium, Equanil, Miltown, Serax, Tranxene, Zanax, Pentobarbital, Librium, Methaqualone, Special K (animal tranquilizer)

Drying Out . . . . Abandon drug habit (Also: Kick, Cleaning Up Act, Cold Turkey (when a user quits without help or other drugs)

Ecstasy . . . . Designer Drugs (Ecstasy, analogs) (Also: XTC, Eve, STP, DOB, MDA, MDMA, MMDA, MDEA, MPTP, MPPP, PEPAP, TMA, PMA)

Feds. . . . . Federal narcotics agents (Also: Wally Narc, Sam)

Five-o . . . . $50 purchase of drugs, typically rock cocaine (Also: Two-o, etc.)

Fix. . . . . Injection of narcotics

Grass . . . . Marijuana (Also: Pot, Reefer, Weed, Joint, J, Mary Jane, Bag, Herb, Hay, Tea, Dope, Bud, Sinsemilla, Thai Sticks, Hash, Hashish, Dime, Nickel, Quarter, Smoke, Green, Skunk-Weed, Rope, Acapulco Gold, Panama Red, Mexican Red Hair, Kona Gold, Maui Wowi)

Green . . . . Money (Also: Bread, Coins, Dead Presidents)

Hashish. . . . . More potent form of marijuana made from a concentration of marijuana flower tops. (Also: Hash, Kif, Shish, Ganja, Rope, Leb, Black Russian, Blond Lebanese, Black Afghani)

The Heat . . . . Police (Also: Pigs, The Man, Big John, Cops, Narcs, Fuzz)

Hit. . . . . Single drug dosage; Drag on marijuana cigarette; Purchase drugs in arrest

Hooked . . . . Addicted

Hooker . . . . Prostitute (Also: Working Girl, Strawberry, Hos, Whore, Street Walker, Lady of the Night, Turning Tricks)

Hot . . . . Wanted by police

Hot shot . . . . Fatal or potentially fatal drug dosage (Also: Overdose, OD)

I'm holding/serving . . . . I have drugs; can make a deal

I'm looking to cop . . . . . I wish to buy

Jim Jones . . . . Marijuana cigarette laced with cocaine and dipped in PCP

Junkie . . . . Drug addict (Also: Hype)

Loaded . . . . Intoxicated by drugs, including alcohol (Also: High, Wasted, Stoned, Cranked, Slammed, Nodding, On the Nod, Smashed, Down, Spacing, Wired, Hammered, Blitzed, Speeding, Flying, Messed Up, Bombed, Banged Up, Shot Up, Jacked Up, Tore Up, Wired, Tweeked, Amped Out, Fried, Right, Straight)

Locked Up . . . . To be in jail (Also: Boxed, Canned, Jailed)

Mainlining . . . . Injecting drugs directly into vein (Also: Shooting, Banging, Geezing, Hitting Home, Registering, Hyping)

Mouth Holding. . . . . . Drugs packaged in balloons and hidden in mouth from police

Mule. . . . . One who sells or transports for a regular peddler (Also: Runner, Carrier, Pigeon)

Nickel Bag . . . . $5 purchase of drugs

Outfit . . . . Equipment for narcotics injection (Also: Fit, Kit, Gizmo, Dropper, Works, Toys, Cooker, Point, Spike, Tie-Off/Tie-Rag)

Pass Out . . . . Lose consciousness from drugs (Also: Black Out, Tube)

PCP . . . . Phencyclidine (Also: Angel Dust, Hog, Lovely, Love Boat, Sherms, Wac, Crystal, Ozone, Dusters, Water, Stick, Wet One, Seems, Super Kool, Killer Weed)

Poly-User . . . . Users who combine two or more drugs to counteract or heighten the effects of the first drug. (For example, see: Blue-Velvet, Caviar and Champagne, Space Basing, Speed Ball, T's and B's, and Jim Jones.)

Quarter bag . . . . $25 purchase of drugs

Rush. . . . . Physical sensations after taking drugs (Also: Flash, High, Bang, Hit Home, Register)

Script . . . . Prescription

Smack. . . . . Heroin (including narcotics and prescription drugs). (Also: H, Harry, Horse, Junk, Powder, Snow, Stuff, Boy, China White, C-and-W, Balloon, Dope, White, Brown, Mud, Gum,

Chiva, Black Tar, Spoons, Papers, Tar;—
other narcotics and prescription drugs used
in place of heroine: Dolophine, Methadone,
Amidone, Codeine, Pectoral Syrup, Percocet,
Pethidine, Talwin, Mepergan, Percodan,
Lomitil, Paregoric, Darvon, Parepectolin,
Fentanyl)

Smokes . . . . Tobacco (nicotine) (Also: Cigarettes, Chew,
Cigars, Puffs, Snuff)

Snitch . . . . Informer (Also: Rat, Gonner, Dead Man)

Source. . . . . Drug Supplier (Also: Dealer, Pusher, Dope
Man, Dope Lady)

Spacebasing . . . . Combination of rock or crack cocaine with
PCP (Also: Whacking)

Speed Ball . . . . Combination of heroin and cocaine or other
amphetamines (Also: Goof Ball)

STP . . . . An hallucinogen (mescaline, peyote, psilocy-
bin, etc.) (Also: Mesc, Buttons, Cactus, Magic
Mushrooms, Mushrooms, Shrooms, Boom-
ers, DMT)

Strawberry . . . . Prostitute (see Hooker) who works for cocaine

THC. . . . . Active ingredient in marijuana and hashish

T's and B's . . . . Combination of Pentazocine and Tripelenna-
mine (Also: T's and Blues)

Uppers . . . . A stimulant (amphetamines, methamphet-
amines, dextroamphetamines, and Ritalin)
(Also: Crystal, Crank, Speed, Fast, Go-Fast,
Peanut Butter Crystal, Yellow, Cross Tops,
White Tops, Hearts, Benzedrine, Bennies,
Co-Pilots, Dexedrine, Dexies, Peaches,
Whites, Whities, LA Turnabouts, Black Beau-
ties, Crystal Meth, Mother's Little Helpers,
Preludin, Bumble Bees, Footballs, Biphetam-
ine, Lid Poppers, Wake Ups, Popping Uppers,
Speeding, Being Wired, Flying, Pre-state,
Didrex, Voranil, Tenuate, Tepanil, Pondimin,
Sanorex, Plegine, Ionamin)

Vapors . . . . Inhalants (solvents, glue, gases, nitrous oxide, amyl and butyl nitrite, hydrocarbons, chlorogydrocarbons) (Also: Honk, Laughing Gas, Glue, Aerosol, Gunk, Locker Room, Buzz Bombs, Bolt, Whippets, Rush, Poppers, Snappers, Whip Cream, Climax)

Zig Zag . . . . Brand of cigarette paper used to roll marijuana smokes

NOTES

Chapter 1. The Challenge

1. Dr. Luther Woodward, with Morton Edwards, editor, *Your Child from Two to Five* (New York: Permabooks, 1955).

2. Dr. James C. Dobson, *The Strong-Willed Child* (Wheaton: Tyndale House Publishers, Inc., 1978), p. 55.

3. John B. Watson & R. R. Watson, *Psychological Care of Infant and Child* (Norton & Company, 1928), pp. 81–82, 87.

Chapter 4. Questions and Answers

1. Dr. James Dobson, *The Strong-Willed Child* (Wheaton: Tyndale House Publishers, Inc. 1978), p. 52.

Chapter 5. The Miracle Tools, Part 1

1. Dr. James Dobson, *Hide and Seek* (Old Tappan, NJ: Fleming H. Revell Company, 1974), p. 69.

Chapter 6. The Miracle Tools, Part 2

1. Dr. James Dobson, *The Strong-Willed Child* (Wheaton: Tyndale House Publishers, Inc., 1978), p. 136.

Chapter 7. Discipline in Learning

1. Jerry Adler, "Creating Problems," *Newsweek* (Fall/Winter 1990) Special Issue, p. 16.

2. Tom Morganthau, "The Future Is Now," *Newsweek* (Fall/Winter 1990), Special Issue, p. 72.

3. *Newsweek,* October 14, 1991, p. 14.

4. Jonathan Kozol, *Illiterate America* (New York: Anchor Press/Doubleday, 1985).

5. *The World Almanac and Book of Facts: 1991,* (New York: Pharos Books, 1990)

6. Dr. Sheldon Glueck & Eleanor T. Glueck, *Unraveling Juvenile Delinquency* (Commonwealth Fund, 1950).

Chapter 8. The Barriers to Learning, Part 1

1. Sources include the following:

Ray, Brian D. "A nationwide study of home education: Family characteristics, legal matters, and student achievement." (1990, available from the National Home Education Research Institute, c/o Western Baptist College, 5000 Deer Park Dr. SE, Salem, OR 97301)

Ray, Brian D. "Home education in North Dakota: Family characteristics and student achievement." (1991, available from the National Home Education Research Institute.)

Ray, Brian D. "Home education in Oklahoma: Family characteristics, student achievement, and policy matters." (1991, available from the National Home Education Research Institute).

2. Sources include the following:

Ray, Brian D. "A nationwide study of home education; family characteristics, legal matters, and student achievement." (1990, available from the National Home Education Research Institute, c/o Western Baptist College, 5000 Deer Park Dr. SE, Salem, OR 97301)

Greene, Sue S. "Home study in Alaska: A profile of K–12 students in the Alaska Centralized Correspondence Study Program." ERIC Document Reproduction Service No. ED 255 494

Ray, Brian D. and Jon Wartes. "The academic achievement and affective development of home-schooled children." *Home Schooling:*

Polictical, Historical, and Pedagogical Perpectives. (Norwood, N.J.: Ablex Publishing Corporation, 1991).

Rakestraw, Jennie F. "Home Schooling in Alabama." *Home School Researcher.* 4(4), 1988, 1–6.

Wartes, Jon. "Five years of home-school testing within Washington state." (December 1991, available from the Washington Home-School Research Project at 15109 N.E. 169 Pl., Woodinville, WA, 98072).

3. Montgomery, Linda R. "The effect of home schooling on the leadership skills of home-schooled students." *Home School Researcher.* 5(1), 1–10.

4. Sources include the following:

   Aikin, Wilfred. *The Story of the Eight Year Study.* 4 vols. (New York: Harper, 1942).

   Delahooke, Mona Maarse. "Home educated children's social/emotional adjustment and academic achievement: A comparative study." Unpublished doctoral dissertation, California School of Professional Psychology, Los Angeles, CA.

   Montgomery, Linda R. "The effect of home schooling on the leadership skills of home-schooled students." *Home School Researcher.* 5(1), 1–10.

5. Dr. James C. Dobson, *The Strong-Willed Child* (Wheaton: Tyndale House Publishers, Inc., 1978), p. 158–160.

Chapter 9. The Barriers to Learning, Part 2

1. Mona Behan, "What Do You Say to a C?" *Parenting Magazine,* April 1992, p. 47.

2. Dr. James C. Dobson, *The Strong-Willed Child* (Wheaton: Tyndale House Publishers, Inc., 1978), p. 158–160.

Chapter 10. Discipline in Morality

1. Gabriel Escobar, "Slayings in Washington Hit New High, 436, for 3rd year," *Washington Post,* November 24, 1990.

2. Steven Manning, "A National Emergency," *Scholastic Update,* April 5, 1991, p. 2.

3. Gordon Witkin, "Kids Who Kill," *U.S. News & World Report,* April 8, 1991, p. 27.

4. Karl Zinsmeister, "Growing Up Scared," *Atlantic Monthly,* June 1990, p. 50.

5. Zinsmeister, "Growing Up Scared," p. 50

6. "Alcohol Use and Abuse in America," *Gallup Report,* No. 265, October 1987, p. 3.

7. Barbara R. Lorch and Robert H. Hughes, "Church Youth, Alcohol and Drug Education Programs, and Youth Substance Use," *Journal of Alcohol and Drug Education*, Vol. 33, No. 2, Winter 1988, p. 15.

8. *Guidelines for Comprehensive Sexuality Education,* National Guidelines Task Force, Sex Information and Education Council of the U.S., 1991.

9. Pamela McDonnell, Sexually Transmitted Diseases Division, Centers for Disease Control, U.S. Dept. of Health & Human Services, t.i., March 16, 1992.

10. Scott W. Wright, "1 in 100 tested at UT has AIDS virus," *Austin American Statesman,* July 14, 1991, p. A14. The federally funded study was based on a nonrandom sample.

11. "Heterosexual HIV Transmission Up in the United States," *American Medical News* (Feb. 3, 1992): 35.

12. U.S. Dept. of Health & Human Services, Public Health Service, Centers for Disease Control, 1991 Division of STD/HIV Prevention *Annual Report,* p.13.

13. Health & Human Services *Annual Report,* p.13.

14. McDonnell

15. Health & Human Services *Annual Report,* p.13.

16. Health & Human Services *Annual Report,* p.13.

17. Health & Human Services *Annual Report,* p.13.

18. Robert E. Johnson et al., "A Seroepidemiologic Survey of the Prevalence of Herpes Simplex Virus Type 2 Infection in the United States," *New England Journal of Medicine,* 321 (July 6, 1989): 7–12.

19. Health & Human Services *Annual Report,* p.13.

20. C. Kuehn and F. Judson, "How common are sexually transmitted infections in adolescents?" *Clinical Practice Sexuality* 5 (1989): 19–25; as cited by Sandra D. Gottwald et al., Profile: Adolescent Ob/Gyn Patients at the University of Michigan, 1989, *The American Journal of Gynecologic Health* 5 (May/June 1991), 23.

21. Kay Stone, Sexually Transmitted Diseases Division, Centers for Disease Control, U.S. Dept. of Health & Human Services, t.i., March 20, 1992.

22. Elise F. Jones and Jacqueline Darroch Forrest, "Contraceptive Failure in the United States: Revised Estimates from the 1982 National Survey of Family Growth," *Family Planning Perspectives* 21 (May/June 1989): 103.

23. Jones and Forrest, "Contraceptive Failure," p. 105.

24. Lode Wigersma and Ron Oud, "Safety and Acceptability of Condoms for Use by Homosexual Men as a Prophylactic Against

Transmission of HIV during Anogenital Sexual Intercourse," *British Medical Journal* 295 (July 11, 1987): 94.

25. Marcia F. Goldsmith, "Sex in the Age of AIDS Calls for Common Sense and Condom Sense," *Journal of the American Medical Association* 257 (May 1, 1987): 2262.

26. Susan G. Arnold et al., "Latex Gloves Not Enough to Exclude Viruses," *Nature* 335 (Sept. 1, 1988): 19.

27. Nancy E. Dirubbo, "The Condom Barrier," *American Journal of Nursing,* Oct. 1987, p. 1306.

28. Theresa Crenshaw, from remarks made at the National Conference on HIV, Washington, D.C., Nov. 15–18, 1991.

29. "Condom Roulette," *Washington Watch* 3 (Washington: Family Research Council, Jan. 1992), p. 1.

30. William D. Mosher and James W. McNally, "Contraceptive Use at First Premarital Intercourse: United States, 1965–1988." *Family Planning Perspectives* 23 (May/June 1991): 111.

31. Cheryl D. Hayes, ed., *Risking the Future: Adolescent Sexuality, Pregnancy and Childbearing* (Washington: National Academy Press, 1987), pp. 46–49.

32. Planned Parenthood poll, "American Teens Speak: Sex, Myths, TV and Birth Control" (New York: Louis Harris & Associates, Inc., 1986), p. 24.

33. "Condom Roulette," *In Focus* 25 (Washington: Family Research Council, Feb. 1992), p. 2.

34. Gilbert L. Crouse, Office of Planning and Evaluation, U.S. Dept. of Health & Human Services, t.i., March 12, 1992, based on data from Planned Parenthood's Alan Guttmacher Institute. Increase calculated from 1973, first year of legal abortion.

35. U.S. Congress, House Committee on Energy and Commerce, Subcommittee on Health and the Environment, "The Reauthorization of Title X of the Public Health Service Act" (testimony submitted by Charmaine Yoest), 102nd Congress, 2nd session, March 19, 1991, p. 2.

36. Margaret A. Fischl et al., "Heterosexual Transmission of Human Immunodeficiency Virus (HIV): Relationship of Sexual Practices to Seroconversion," III International Conference on AIDS, June 1–5, 1987, Abstracts Volume, p. 178.

37. U.S. Dept. of Health & Human Services, National Centers for Health Statistics, Centers for Disease Control, "Percent of Women 15–19 Years of Age Who Are Sexually Experienced, by Race, Age and Marital Status: United States, 1988," National Survey of Family Growth.

38. Joseph S. McIlhaney, Jr., M.D., *Sexuality and Sexually Transmitted Diseases* (Grand Rapids: Baker Book House, 1990), p. 137.

39. A.M.B. Goldstein and Susan M. Garabedian-Ruffalo, "A Treatment Update to Resistant Gonorrhea," *Medical Aspects of Human Sexuality,* (August 1991): 39.

40. Reprinted with permission by Word Publishing. Dr. James C. Dobson and Gary L. Bauer, *Children at Risk* (Dallas: Word Publishing, 1990), pp. 11–13.

41. Reprinted with permission by *USA Today*. Kim Painter, "AIDS Surging Among Teens," *USA Today,* April 13, 1992.

42. Dr. Joe McIlhaney, "A Doctor Speaks Out on Sexually Transmitted Diseases" (Colorado Springs: Focus on the Family).

43. S. R. Kellert and A. R. Felthouse. "Childhood cruelty toward animals among criminals and noncriminals." *Human Relations* 38 (1985): 1113–1129.

44. A. R. Felthous and S. R. Kellert, "Childhood cruelty to animals and later aggression against people: A review," *American Journal of Psychiatry,* (1987),pp. 144, 710–717.

Chapter 11. A Moment for Mom

1. Reprinted with permission by Randall Pearson. Mrs. Alice Pearson, "Are All the Children In?" *Heartspun and Homespun Poems* (Adventure Publications, 1982).

Appendix

1. Sources include the following:

Pomona, California, Police Department

Los Angeles, California, Police Department

Denver, Colorado, Police Department

Colorado Springs, Colorado, Police Department

Drug & Alcohol Treatment Program, El Paso County, Colorado, Health Department

U.S. Department of Justice, Drug Enforcement Administration, San Diego, California, Field Division

Stephen Arterburn & Jim Burns, *Drug Proof Your Kids* (Focus on the Family Publishing, 1989).

Growing up Drug Free: A Parent's Guide to Prevention, U.S. Dept of Education, Washington, D.C., 1990.

Additional titles from Dr. James Dobson

The New Dare to Discipline also available on Tyndale Living Audio
0-8423-7429-9

DISCIPLINE WITH LOVE   0-8423-0665-X
Excerpts from the classic *Dare to Discipline*.

DR. DOBSON ANSWERS YOUR QUESTIONS   0-8423-0580-7
Responses to common questions about home and family.

**DR. DOBSON ANSWERS YOUR QUESTIONS:
CONFIDENT FAMILIES**   0-8423-1105-X
Practical advice on anger, depression, self-esteem, and more.

**DR. DOBSON ANSWERS YOUR QUESTIONS:
MARRIAGE & SEXUALITY**   0-8423-1106-8
Practical advice on romance, conflict, gender differences, and more.

**DR. DOBSON ANSWERS YOUR QUESTIONS:
RAISING CHILDREN**   0-8423-1104-1
Practical advice on spirituality, adolescence, discipline, and more.

THE STRONG-WILLED CHILD   0-8423-5924-9
Learn to discipline a child without breaking his spirit.

**WHAT WIVES WISH THEIR HUSBANDS KNEW ABOUT
WOMEN**   0-8423-7896-0
Wise, humorous insights for both spouses on marital happiness.

WHEN GOD DOESN'T MAKE SENSE   0-8423-8227-5
An assurance of God's constant care when circumstances are beyond our
control.
   Large print edition   0-8423-8242-9
   When God Doesn't Make Sense study guide   0-8423-8239-9
   Available on Tyndale Living Audio   0-8423-7430-2